"This is a Kingdom book. A much-ne
masterful work, *Abiding in His Presence*, will revolutionize how you
think, speak, pray, and live. Both authors are gifted students and
teachers of God's Word, and their passion and teaching style dwell
in every book they write.

"After reading *Abiding in His Presence*, you will agree that the revelation and empowerment held within these pages have the potential
to wreck your life (for the good) and position you to live where you
were created to live, in His Presence! *Abiding in His Presence* should
be on the bookshelf of every leader in all walks of life. Among other
things, it's a road map for empowering and releasing the next generation into purpose.

"Thank you, Alemu and Chuck, for writing this book. We will
use it at Kingdom University."

Dr. Greg Hood, Th.D., president, Kingdom University;
author, *Rebuilding the Broken Altar: Awakening
out of Chaos*; www.GregHood.org

"These authors' passion to see the hearts and minds of all believers
filled with the revelatory understanding of the Lord drives them to
write such incredible books, like this one.

"*Abiding in His Presence* is written as a guide to show how each
and every one of us has a call to see the Lord truly manifest Himself
in our lives, so we can establish our eternal relationship with Him.
By learning how to walk with the Lord like Enoch, David, and many
others, we can begin to understand our truest nature and how to
shape our future.

"*Abiding in His Presence* will not only teach you how to link your
godly desires to your faith, so you can rebuild and sanctify an altar
to the Lord in your heart, but it will also teach you how to know
Him as a friend."

Simon Lyons, director of media and presentation,
Global Spheres/Glory of Zion

"I have worked with Dr. Alemu Beeftu for many years and have read all of his books. He is one of the greatest writers and teachers, especially when it comes to the heart of the matter, which is our spiritual walk with God, Jesus, and the Holy Spirit. The spiritual depth and truth of his messages are encouraging, uplifting, and even challenging.

"In this collaboration with Chuck D. Pierce, *Abiding in His Presence*, Dr. Beeftu presents the importance of our relationship with God. You'll read, 'The Lord Jesus Christ came to dwell among us, to save us and dwell in us for everything in every day.' God has always wanted a relationship with His creation. Together, these two authors teach us in detail how our salvation (relationship) is the key to experiencing the complete and total victory Christ died to give us. The Word states that apart from Him, we can do nothing (see John 15:5). That means *we need to abide in His presence*.

"In this book, you'll also read many references to the men of God who completed what God called them to do because of His presence in their lives. Moses discovered the power of His presence, and it's time for all of us, the Body of Christ, to walk in it as well. I encourage you to read this book!"

Polly Harder, author and speaker; president, R.H. Publishing

ABIDING
IN HIS
PRESENCE

ABIDING IN HIS PRESENCE

The Secret to Waging War and Bearing Fruit

Chuck D. Pierce
and Alemu Beeftu

Chosen

a division of Baker Publishing Group
Minneapolis, Minnesota

© 2024 by Alemu Beeftu and Chuck D. Pierce

Published by Chosen Books
Minneapolis, Minnesota
www.chosenbooks.com

Chosen Books is a division of
Baker Publishing Group, Grand Rapids, Michigan

Printed in the United States of America

ISBN 978-0-8007-7243-7 (paper)
ISBN 978-0-8007-7244-4 (casebound)
ISBN 978-1-4934-4536-3 (ebook)

Library of Congress Control Number: 2023033774

24 25 26 27 28 29 30   7 6 5 4 3 2 1

INVITATION

Throughout human history, God has been looking for individuals whose heart is after His. Those with His heart are able to establish an extraordinary covenantal relationship to reveal the fullness of His glory.

Today, God is preparing and positioning the remnant to walk and dwell in His presence to restore their reflection of His glory. He is raising the remnant to abide in His presence and make known the power of His redemption through the power of the Gospel.

The purpose of this book is to highlight the process of walking with God, committing to His purpose wholeheartedly, and understanding the covenant relationship required to remain in His presence. These principles allow us to correct the past and shape the future, in order for the greater glory to be revealed.

- Do you have the desire to dwell in His presence?
- Do you have a passion to fulfill His purpose in your life with the power and anointing of the Holy Spirit?
- Do you have the longing to overcome the deception of the enemy in your life in order to abide in His presence?

This book is for you!

CONTENTS

FOREWORD

When I was a younger man, I had the privilege of encountering a great woman of God by the name of Kathryn Kuhlman. I had never seen anyone like her before, and I would be greatly influenced by her ministry. Working in her miracle meetings, I had many opportunities to witness powerful, and often dramatic, healings. I have heard many people say over the years, "Kathryn Kuhlman must surely have had a gift of healing!" However, after observing Ms. Kuhlman and her ministry for several years, I came to a different conclusion about her giftings. I think her primary gift was not healing, but hosting. She had such an ability to *abide in His presence.* She had somehow discovered that if she could provide an environment and moment for the Holy Spirit to enter and feel welcomed, He would come, and that was when the miracles would happen.

I recall that most of the healing miracles happened for people when they were simply sitting in God's presence in those meetings, during the times of worship and the preaching of His Word. In His presence, it was easier for people to simply believe, and then the miracle came. *After* they were healed in His presence, they would come to the altar, where doctors and other workers would interview them and verify their healing. They would then be brought onto the stage to give their testimony, and Ms. Kuhlman would pray and give all glory to God for what He had done. She taught us that

"God never separates His power from His presence." How correct she was! Her skill at learning to abide in His presence would always result in His power working.

After one of her meetings in Fort Worth, Texas, Ms. Kuhlman was walking from the stage back to her dressing room to get some much-needed rest. She noticed me standing with a friend of mine backstage. She stopped and turned to walk toward us . . . and then we both realized she was coming to pray for us. I think I heard the Lord speak to me, asking what I would like to receive from Him when Ms. Kuhlman prayed for me. He asked, *Would you like a gift of healing to serve Me with?*

Without hesitation, I replied, "No, Sir. I would like a gift of hosting."

Ms. Kuhlman prayed the most humble and powerful prayer for my friend and me. I believe God answered her prayer, and the seed of a gift of hosting was graciously planted in my life at that moment, which continues to grow to this day.

When I read *Abiding in His Presence* by Chuck D. Pierce and Dr. Alemu Beeftu, I immediately knew several things. First, this book would prove to be one of the most strategic and timely books they have written, addressing a key issue in the hour we live in—not only about hosting God's presence, but about *how* we prepare ourselves to host Him. I knew this book would be a significant means God would use to prepare the Body of Christ for a great end-time revival. I knew it would help us steward a sweeping move of the Holy Spirit across the nations.

When the Philistines did not know *how* to host the Ark of God's presence, and even King David failed by not following God's protocols on *how* to host the Ark, God raised up a man named Obed Edom, who knew *how* to welcome and host His presence. And all that he had was blessed (see 2 Samuel 6:11–12). *Abiding in His Presence* by Chuck D. Pierce and Alemu Beeftu will prepare you with the keys to be an effective host of God's presence. And all that *you* have will be blessed!

Don Crum, Leadership International

INTRODUCTION

Dwelling in His Presence

ALEMU BEEFTU

Dwelling in the presence of God is the core of our justification and hope for eternal glorification. God's desire is to fellowship with us, as well as to dwell among His people. The Lord Jesus Christ came to dwell among us, to save us and dwell in us for everything in every day. John tells us that "God lives in us and his love is made complete in us" (1 John 4:12). That's what the Lord Jesus promised the disciples: "If anyone loves Me, he will keep My word; and My Father will love him, and We will come to him and make Our home with him" (John 14:23 NKJV).

Therefore, being able to dwell in the presence of God's glory starts with a relationship with Him through our salvation, when we become His children by accepting and welcoming Him into our lives. At salvation, we receive the seal of the Holy Spirit, "who is the guarantee of our inheritance until the redemption of the purchased possession, to the praise of His glory" (Ephesians 1:14 NKJV). Because of the Holy Spirit dwelling in us, we call God Almighty "Abba,

Father!" From this initial starting point, we continue the transformation of becoming like Him through the work of the Holy Spirit. It is an ongoing daily relationship with our Lord and Savior.

Abiding in God's presence starts with establishing our eternal relationship with Him as our Creator, King, Savior, and Father. Understanding and fully accepting this truth of who He is in our lives changes our attitude, actions, and lifestyle.

We then demonstrate hosting God's presence in the following ways. First is having a determination to walk with God by being set apart. The substance of holiness is to be set apart to God. It is written,

> Come out from among them
> And be separate, says the Lord.
> Do not touch what is unclean,
> And I will receive you.
> I will be a Father to you,
> And you shall be My sons and daughters,
> Says the LORD Almighty.
>
> 2 Corinthians 6:17–18 NKJV

The first person who learned to dwell in the presence of God by walking with Him was Enoch. In his walk with God, he totally became God's and was not for anything else. That's the sign of abiding in Him, when we are lost in His glorious presence. The Lord made Enoch His own. Enoch didn't come back to earth to die a natural death. "Enoch walked faithfully with God; then he was no more, because God took him away" (Genesis 5:24). Therefore, abiding in the presence of God is more than attending religious activities or singing spiritual songs; it is having an ongoing relationship with Him by dwelling in His presence.

Second, dwelling in His presence is demonstrated by a total commitment to live for His will and purpose. We can't abide in God's presence without our willingness to pay the necessary price by obeying daily His revealed will as His messengers on earth. The Lord Jesus Christ demonstrated this eternal truth when He came into the world and said,

> Sacrifice and offering you did not desire, but a body you prepared for me; with burnt offerings and sin offerings you were not pleased. Then I said, "Here I am—it is written about me in the scroll—I have come to do your will, O God."
>
> Hebrews 10:5–7

Dwelling in God's presence includes a willingness to become the messenger of God for the salvation of others.

Third, hosting His presence is demonstrated by a willingness to walk in covenant relationship with God, becoming a friend of God, just like Abraham. Without understanding and accepting God's covenant relationship, it is impossible to abide in His presence. This relationship moves us from where we have been to where we should be, as well as including the circumcision of our heart, which is part of preparing a place for His presence. To receive His presence in our covenant relationship demands that we enter into our covenant inheritance by believing in and obeying the Word of the Lord, and by believing in His promises. Each of us has a prophetic destiny that is God's call on our life. Entering into our prophetic destiny requires a walk of faith, since without faith it is impossible to please God. Abraham, the father of faith, followed God to a place he would later receive as his inheritance, and he built an altar of worship. We establish a lasting covenant too, and remain in God's presence as His friend.

Fourth, hosting and abiding in His presence means being among the remnant who seek His face persistently. King David cried out to God, "My heart says of you, 'Seek his face!' Your face, LORD, I will seek" (Psalm 27:8).

The only way we can secure God's presence is by keeping our fire of love and worship burning, as well as keeping our altar pure. That means maintaining divine order—where God's altar is kept pure and worship fire is alive for His presence to dwell in, where the revelation of His Word can be released, where His light will shine, and where the power of the Gospel is demonstrated.

The primary goal of this book is to show the importance of abiding in God's presence in order to advance His Kingdom on earth. We are to bring back the centrality of the presence of Christ in very practical and applicable ways for every believer, and for the Body of Christ at large.

If you have a desire to know Him in a deeper way and walk with Him, even to the extent that you forget yourself in His presence and live as the messenger of God on earth, this book is the starting point for you. Read it and apply it! Your covenant relationship with God will impact your generation and will glorify Him.

1

THE WAR TO ABIDE

CHUCK D. PIERCE

He who dwells in the secret place of the Most High shall abide under the shadow of the Almighty.

Psalm 91:1 NKJV

In a chaotic world that has multiple influences on our life, we talk so much about warfare. Warfare is defined as conflict. Warfare can create chaos. However, the proper definition of warfare is the grace to fight and have victory.

In battle, I have always seen the greatest war of contention is over our abiding place. This book is about abiding. Throughout *Abiding in His Presence*, we show you keys in your daily war, how to face conflicts, and really, how to abide. The enemy of your soul, your adversary the devil, has one goal: to keep you from getting into your abiding place. And if you do succeed in entering, his goal is to make sure to pull you from your abiding place.

In the midst of this changing world, always remember that change in your life produces a new, enlarged place. The enemy desires to hold you captured or confined to your present place, of course, and that place might even be good. But it might not be God's best, and He may be calling you to enlarge the place of your tent (see Isaiah 54:2). Once you are "enlarged," you must increase your security level. The abiding place is linked with your security.

Actually, the Bible defines this as our abiding place:

> He who dwells in the secret place of the Most High shall abide under the shadow of the Almighty. I will say of the LORD, "He is my refuge and my fortress; my God, in Him I will trust."
>
> Surely He shall deliver you from the snare of the fowler and from the perilous pestilence. He shall cover you with His feathers.
>
> Psalm 91:1–4 NKJV

If you abide in Him:

1. Your fears are relieved, your dread of darkness is removed, and you no longer resist your path ahead.
2. You stop fretting over what the wicked in the world are doing. That becomes the Lord's problem, and you are relieved from the worry of judgment.
3. You don't fear plagues like the COVID pandemic.
4. You no longer hide from the snakes, cobras, lions, and other demonic influences on your path ahead.
5. You feel God's love.
6. You laugh when trouble surrounds you.
7. The dreaded sting of death is gone.

This speaks of the great protection we can enjoy by being in the right place at the right time. Amid bioterrorism warnings, flu epidemics, and threats, Psalm 91 brings great solace.

Securing Your Portion in Days Ahead

In my very first book with Rebecca Wagner Sytsema, *Possessing Your Inheritance*, we shared this about security:

> To "secure" means to put beyond the hazard of losing. It means to bring something to a place of hope or safety; to be fastened, planted and established. When we secure something, we have removed it from exposure to danger. Secure also means to have a feeling of trust or confidence. When we don't have confidence, we have lost a place of security within us. But God longs to fasten us in a secure place.
>
> As Matthew 6:19 reminds us, our security does not come from treasures stored up for ourselves here on earth where moth and rust destroy and thieves break in and steal—or where the stock market can crash. Our security must be firmly fastened in God. When we have that in order, then we can secure our inheritance. That does not mean we will never experience any loss. . . . But it does mean that anything we have has been given to us by God, and as long as we position ourselves correctly in the Lord, the inheritance God has for us is securely fastened in Him.[1]

Isaiah 22:23 (NKJV) says, "I will fasten him as a peg in a secure place." Where we live and why we live there are both part of our abiding, or security. My wife, Pam, moved from place to place as a child. Eventually, her family fell apart and she was adopted into a military family that moved from place to place. She had to become secure by developing an understanding of what real security meant. We can separate our spiritual abiding place from our physical abiding place, but touching God in the physical habitat is key to our lives being free from anxiety. Acts 17:26 says that He predetermines the place where you are to seek Him. In His goodness, He helps each of us seek and find the best place He has prepared for our fullness. In that predetermined physical place, you will begin to find Him spiritually and gain the strategy necessary to secure your portion.

In our book *One Thing: How to Keep Your Faith in a World of Chaos*, Pam and I shared this list of seven key points on how to secure your new enlarged place:

1. THINK differently! Let new ways of thinking about yourself and those that you are aligned with develop.
2. Make any changes necessary in developing skills that will help you advance.
3. Receive MERCY and GRACE to get beyond any failures or faults from your past that hold you captive and make you feel condemned.
4. FORGIVE and release anyone so you are fully released to advance into the best ahead. Forgiveness breaks all the schemes of the enemy.
5. BREAK the power that pulls you back into an old, comfortable place or form of worship. Find creative ways to prosper in your new place instead of longing for the securities of your past.
6. Do not let fear and unbelief keep you from entering into WAR for the fulfillment of your destiny.
7. RECEIVE THE BANNER FOR YOUR FUTURE. His Banner over you is Love. Let Jehovah Nissi arise in your midst.[2]

Come into your new place and let all mistrust and wounds from the past remain in the old place you vacated.

War from Your Abiding Place

There are so many enemies on our path. Someone asked me once, "Do you see demons behind every bush?"

I stated, "I see at least 10. However, if there are no demons on *my* path and no demons in *my* sphere of authority, I keep walking."

I never war just to war. I only go to war when I cannot get in my abiding place. Or only when, once I'm in my abiding place, the enemy attempts to remove me from that place of rest, protection, and trust the Almighty has allowed me to experience.

Because one of the key strategies of our enemy in warfare is to disrupt our abiding place, we must understand time. God gave His covenant to us in time. In restoring order in the chaos, He worked six days and then "shabbated." The Sabbath is linked with the abiding place of God. Therefore, if we get out of rest even in times of war, then we can make wrong decisions that can keep God's blessings from manifesting.

In Jewish culture, there is a prayer called *Havdalah* that is prayed at the end of Sabbath. It means "difference." The prayer distinguishes the difference between the sacred (Shabbat) and the profane (the other six days). During this prayer, a cup is filled to overflowing with wine as a symbol that the Shabbat blessings will spill into the week. Another important aspect of this observance is breathing in from a container of aromatic leaves or spices. This signifies that the aroma of holiness will follow into and sweeten the new week.

Being at the right place at the right time in Him is also a key to remaining in our abiding place. When you are at the right place at the right time, you see circumspectly. Ephesians 5:15–16 (NKJV) says, "See then that you walk circumspectly, not as fools but as wise, redeeming the time, because the days are evil." If we walk in our abiding place, then we are always redeeming time.

Time is a circle. You are redeeming your past, you are walking victoriously in your present, and you can gain perspective for your future. Jeremiah 29:11 (AMP) says, "'For I know the plans and thoughts that I have for you,' says the LORD, 'plans for peace and well-being and not for disaster, to give you a future and a hope.'" The Lord desires our expected end to be a good future!

Filled with the Holy Spirit

We are made in God's image body, soul, and spirit. The Holy Spirit inhabits our human spirit and connects us to the heavenly abiding place that God has prepared for us. It is in this abiding place that the Lord will reveal His wisdom to us.

The Holy Spirit is also the one who reveals God's will to us and empowers us to accomplish it. He is our helper. When we cry out for help, we are crying out for a manifestation of His presence. And in His presence, we will gain the wisdom and understanding needed to overthrow the enemy in our lives.

One time the Lord spoke this word to me because of all the chaos that was going on around me: *I am giving grace for the divine interruptions that happen to My people, where they have made missteps and Satan came in to rob. But because you have endured what I told you to last year, and stayed in joy no matter what you went through, you're going to unravel those old cycles off My people. I will have a joyous people who are prospering in soul and body. If they can restore their prosperity in soul and body, they'll start prospering everywhere I send them! Prosperity is coming. The old cycles are going to break, and I am going to cause My people to rediscover joy, get into and maintain their cycle of joy, and you won't recognize this nation for all the joy. I am going to crisscross this nation, and healing will spring forth because of this joy!*

From Abiding to Abundance

The Lord has a purpose to move any desolation into a new level of abundance. From the beginning, when God saw the earth in confusion and chaos, He planned for a people who would move from chaos into multiplication. He spoke! Chaos subsided, and abundance began. This is the essence of spiritual life. When Yeshua, Jesus of Nazareth, defined why He came or was sent to earth, He said, "I came that they may have and enjoy life, and have it in abundance [to the full, till it overflows]" (John 10:10 AMP).

Many Christians, and even others who are seeking to understand their earthly purpose, never realize that the One who was sent to redeem them purposed them to "enjoy life." Prior to this portion of verse 10, we find Jesus declaring, "I am the Door; anyone who enters through Me will be saved [and will live forever], and will go in and out [freely], and find pasture (spiritual security). The thief comes only in order to steal and kill and destroy" (verses 9–10 AMP). This is meant to help you enter the door (called Christ) into a new dimension of abundance.

We have approximately 75 people who work for Glory of Zion International at the Global Spheres Center. I remember sitting in my office several years ago in a quandary because I knew I needed to give a Christmas bonus for those who had served so faithfully all year long. I know that the holidays can be a tremendous blessing, but can be very stressful as well. I heard the Lord remind me of one of the key verses that has directed my life, the one I just quoted from John 10. His voice illuminated deep within my spirit the portion of that Scripture that says *I came that you might enjoy life.*

I knew I had to move by faith. Faith comes from hearing . . . hearing when the Spirit of God speaks to us. Faith's counterpart is presumption. Therefore, one must be sure one has heard the voice of God. The Spirit of God spoke to me and said, *Enjoy those who have served, and bless them.*

I knew then that I was to give out of our lack and bless each one who had served (see Mark 12:41–44). Joy began to overwhelm me. By the next morning, all I had given (which was a substantial amount) was already on the way through the mail. The real miracle was that something changed in me. Anxiety from trauma that I had carried for years and years and years had lifted. That old, bad friend was gone, and the joy of the Lord had replaced that portion within my soul and spirit.

Warfare is conflict, and in the midst of the conflict we can lose our joy. Joy produces strength. When we don't sense the life of Christ flowing through us, we need to ask the Lord, *What has happened to my passion? In the midst of my circumstance, Lord, did I just get tired and quit withstanding?*

In truth, we can pray until we are green. We can engage in all sorts of religious activities. But if we don't resist the enemy during that trial (the temptation toward passivity and all other temptations), and if we don't let that trial bring the working of the cross into us, then we won't really enter the passion and fullness of life that the Lord has for each of us. Having God's passion as we walk in wisdom and revelation is the key to protecting ourselves from being outwitted by the enemy.

Yeshua Himself prophesied that a triumphant people, filled with the Father's revelation, would arise and prevail against hell's gates. This people will do exploits! They will take resources and multiply or change them into a form to be used today. These people are an apostolic people. They are a modern people who very much look like the people who crossed over the Jordan River 476 years after the time God spoke them into existence when He communicated to their father, Abraham. The gates of hell will not be able to withstand this people. They are people who will build a new prototype for today and unlock a Kingdom mentality that hell cannot withstand. They will have centers for gatherings that are filled with the fire of His glory!

When you read Matthew 16, notice that when the Father revealed to Peter who Yeshua was, a prophecy came forth. Unlocked revelation releases prophecy! Jesus released a prophecy for ages to come:

> Then Jesus answered him, Blessed (happy, fortunate and to be envied) are you, Simon Bar-Jonah. For flesh and blood [men] have not revealed this to you, but My Father Who is in heaven.
>
> And I tell you, you are Peter [Greek, *Petros*—a large piece of rock], and on this rock [Greek, *petra*—a huge rock like Gibraltar] I will build My church, and the gates of Hades (the powers of the infernal region) shall not overpower it [or be strong to its detriment or hold out against it].

I will give you the keys of the kingdom of heaven; and whatever you bind (declare to be improper and unlawful) on earth must be what is already bound in heaven; and whatever you loose (declare lawful) on earth must be what is already loosed in heaven.

Matthew 16:17–19 AMPC

I am honored that I am numbered with this "people of triumph." I came to know the Father of my spirit when I was a maturing youth. He opened the heavenly vault and gave me a glimpse of His blessings when I was a young man. He showed me the war and the army of darkness that was determined to keep me from accessing these blessings. He taught my hands to war and my heart to worship. His voice has become my life. Daily, He is still teaching me to experience why I am here: *to enjoy life!* Daniel and Amber Pierce, my children who lived in Israel for ten years, have written an incredible book called *Joy in the War: Expand Your Ability to Embrace Hope* (Charisma House, 2021). I suggest you get a copy of that book to help you embrace hope in the midst of your warfare.

I have come to know the One who paid the price for my freedom. The Father sacrificed the Son to unlock all spiritual blessings in heavenly places. These blessings have amassed through the years of your bloodline dwelling in the earth. Some of your predecessors may have added to these blessings through their obedience. Some may have accessed the blessings the Father created for them and manifested these blessings on earth. Others may have rejected these blessings and deferred them to your time to be accessed. Whatever the case, He came that you may *enjoy* the *abundance* of His blessings!

Worship: A Key to Our Abiding Place

We are positioned in the heavens, but we walk on earth (see Ephesians 1–2). When we know our abiding place in the heavenlies, we walk with great confidence and faith. We go to war when the enemy tries to pull us out of that abiding place or block us from ascending to it in Christ. We often feel this blockade as we ascend in worship. This is when it's necessary to express the sound of war from our spirits toward the enemy. Remember, we are worshiping all the way into the throne room of God.

There will always be war and conflict. Jesus said,

> And you will hear of wars and rumors of wars. See that you are not troubled; for all these things must come to pass, but the end is not yet. For nation will rise against nation, and kingdom against kingdom. And there will be famines, pestilences, and earthquakes in various places. All these things are the beginning of sorrows.
>
> Matthew 24:6–8 NKJV

However, He also added, "But he who endures to the end shall be saved" (Matthew 24:13 NJKV). To endure is to hold one's ground in conflict and to hold up against adversity. To endure is to stand under stress and, as found in Ephesians 6:11, to stand firm. To endure is to persevere under pressure while we wait calmly and courageously for the Lord to intervene. This is an energetic resistance toward our enemy as we draw near to the Lord and intimately worship Him.

When we remain in our abiding place, we remain pure during the war. The fragrance of God encircles us. Angels are drawn to us. Angelic forces descend to set guard over our mouth and watch over the door of our lips (see Psalm 141:3–4). What is in our heart proceeds out of our mouth. Your speech remains triumphant because you are speaking from a heavenly realm and not just contending here in the earth.

True victory in warfare occurs when we get our feet planted on our enemies. Warfare is not yelling at the devil. It is placing our feet on top of his purposes that are set against our victory and Jesus' influence in the earth. God's intimate relationship with us is secure. We walk faithfully in His ministry in the earth realm. We rule from

His divine government. We accomplish our mission. And we abide in His presence.

QUESTIONS FOR ABIDING DEEPER

- What does security mean to you? Is it a person, a place, or a certain level of accomplishment?
- Did you know that God intends for His children to enjoy life in the midst of war, as well as in times of peace? What does it look like for you to enjoy life during trials?
- Can you recall a time when you were abiding in God's presence? What did that feel like? What was the tangible fruit in your life?

2

WALKING WITH GOD TO ABIDE

Alemu Beeftu

My lover is mine, and I am his.

Song of Solomon 2:16 NLT

God is looking for someone who desires to restore the glory of fellowship by walking with Him. God is the seeker of generations. He lacks nothing. He never had unmet needs. He is the Creator and owner of everything. Furthermore, earth and all its fullness are His. Throughout human history, however, the Lord has always been seeking individuals whose hearts are committed to Him, so He can reveal His purpose and glory to them, as well as through them. It started in the Garden of Eden with Adam and Eve, when He bestowed upon them His glory by creating them in His image.

Since sin entered the world and separated mankind from God, He has continued to look for those whose hearts are after Him. His desire is to save and bring them close to Him as friends so they can become the messengers of His greatness, majesty, kindness, and goodness on earth in every generation.

The apostle Paul wrote, "Yet he has not left himself without testimony: He has shown kindness by giving you rain from heaven and crops in their seasons; he provides you with plenty of food and fills your hearts with joy" (Acts 14:17). God has never stopped looking. His resolve to find the lost caused Him to send His Son, the Lord Jesus Christ, the Word, who became flesh (incarnation). Jesus described His mission on earth this way: "For the Son of Man came to seek and to save the lost" (Luke 19:10).

God Is Looking for Right Hearts

Whom is the Lord looking for in each generation? And why?

The Lord is looking for individuals who would be committed to walking with Him. The Lord is looking for those whose hearts are committed to Him for a personal relationship and fellowship. "For the eyes of the LORD range throughout the earth to strengthen those whose hearts are fully committed to him" (2 Chronicles 16:9).

From Genesis through the New Testament, God's desire was always to have a family and share His name and His nature with them. Paul praises the Lord for this: "For this reason I kneel before the Father, from whom his whole family in heaven and on earth derives its name" (Ephesians 3:14–15). Peter tells us that we have received God's nature to become His family members, "by which have been given to us exceedingly great and precious promises, that through these you may be partakers of the divine nature, having escaped the corruption that is in the world through lust" (2 Peter 1:4 NKJV).

In every generation, God is looking for those who are willing to separate themselves, walk with Him, and testify of the goodness of the Lord in their generation by becoming His friends. These individuals become a witness in their generation by revealing the heart and power of God to redeem. The fact that the Word tells us

"Such is the generation of those who seek him, who seek your face, God of Jacob" (Psalm 24:6) means God is looking and searching for people in every generation who would be set apart to seek Him with passion.

Seeking the Lord with all our heart, soul, and spirit doesn't only draw us to God; it also draws God to us. He qualifies us to receive His grace, mercy, and favor, and this makes us true witnesses of His power to save, restore, and reform. Being a true witness means hearing, seeing, and experiencing God by being in His presence and declaring His glory and marvelous deeds.

Seeing and experiencing makes our testimony credible. "That which was from the beginning, which we have heard, which we have seen with our eyes, which we have looked at and our hands have touched—this we proclaim concerning the Word of life" (1 John 1:1). God is looking in every generation for those who are willing to come close to Him for an extraordinary relationship, to be set apart to walk with Him daily, to hear His voice, to know and follow Him to the end as His own true witnesses. "My sheep listen to my voice; I know them, and they follow me" (John 10:27).

The mark of walking with God is to hear His voice and follow Him wholeheartedly. This means dwelling in His presence and living with Him before we attempt to live for Him. The Lord has looked for this kind of person since sin separated us from Him. In the first search, after the death of Abel (whom Cain murdered because of Abel's worship of God), He found two individuals on the earth. They were Enoch and Noah. *Enoch* means "dedication." *Noah* means "rest." Both were known for walking with God. They came to Him and followed Him, despite the condition of their generation and the world around them. They identified themselves as followers of the true God. In my view, these two were a prophetic picture of what God is looking for in every generation. We'll talk more about Noah in the next chapter, but here, I want to look more closely at how Enoch walked with God.

Becoming His

The first person referred to as "a man who walked with God" was Enoch. As his prophetic name indicated, he was the first person who was dedicated to God wholeheartedly. "Enoch walked faithfully with God; then he was no more, because God took him away" (Genesis 5:24). Enoch walked with God for 300 years, but he lived 365 years. It looks as if something happened to him at age 65 to inspire him not only to walk with God, but to live for his prophetic destiny.

That's a life dedicated to Creator God. Whatever caused Enoch to make that shift in his life brought him to his true calling. The Lord made Enoch his own from that time on for 300 years, until the day He took him home for good. There are twelve marks we can identify on Enoch's life that pleased God. Let's look at each mark individually.

1. Dedication to God. Enoch lived according to his prophetic name. In God's view, a name isn't just a label; it's a description of purpose, true prophetic identity, and our life's calling. Enoch understood and accepted that calling. Our prophetic name is in our identity. When we talk about prophetic names, we are not limited to names that have meaning in specific languages. The meaning comes from God's plan and purpose.

2. Walking with God. Enoch gave up everything to follow God. Walking with God requires holiness and total dedication to the full purpose of God. Enoch willingly separated himself for God to live a holy life. It was not what he did for God, but what he was willing to be for God that made him remarkably special. Walking with God requires full agreement. "Do two men walk together unless they have made an appointment?" (Amos 3:3 AMP).

3. Being surrendered to God. Enoch surrendered to God's will and purpose. Surrender is more than just an agreement with someone on principles; it's a determination to pay the price and not turn back. The Bible doesn't tell us what it cost Enoch to submit to God's plan, but we do know that he didn't want to go back to his old life. This is purposeful determination. We need to protect our relationship with God to keep unity with the Spirit. When Ruth refused to go back to her old life and insisted on remaining with Naomi, she exhibited biblical determination:

> But Ruth replied, "Don't urge me to leave you or to turn back from you. Where you go I will go, and where you stay I will stay. Your people will be my people and your God my God. Where you die I will die, and there I will be buried. May the LORD deal with me, be it ever so severely, if even death separates you and me."
>
> Ruth 1:16–17

Ruth's determination included these factors:

- Decision (*Don't urge me to leave you*)
- Submission (*or to turn back from you*)
- Commitment (*Where you go I will go*)
- Friendship (*where you stay, I will stay*)
- Oneness (*Your people will be my people*)
- Spiritual Unity (*your God my God*)
- Determination (*Where you die I will die*)
- Paying the Price (*there I will be buried*)
- Covenant Relationship (*May the Lord deal with me, be it ever so severely, if even death separates you and me*)

4. Pleasing God. "He was commended as one who pleased God" (Hebrews 11:5). Enoch pleased God by meeting God's desire for fellowship, walking with Him as His own. He pleased God not by his activities or what he did for God, but through his relationship, which God desires more than anything else. That is why the Father in heaven declared about Jesus, "This is my Son, whom I love; with him I am well pleased" (Matthew 3:17). There is no greater declaration in human history than this. That's what God was looking for, until the day Jesus came and fulfilled God's longing.

5. Believing in God. We come into God's family through faith. "For by grace you have been saved through faith" (Ephesians 2:8 NKJV). We live by faith for His glory, as it is written, "The righteous will live by his faith" (Romans 1:17). Enoch became righteous in the eyes of the Lord by faith, and we also please Him by faith. For Enoch, faith was believing what was revealed to him and acting upon it. True faith and trust create sincere movement to advance a cause.

6. Fulfilling God's desire for fellowship. Enoch "walked with God." God's desire was to fellowship with His people, whom He created for His pleasure. God revealed Himself in the Garden for fellowship with Adam and Eve: "Then the man and his wife heard the sound of the LORD God as he was walking in the garden in the cool of the day" (Genesis 3:8). God found in Enoch the fellowship that He had lost in the Garden after the Fall.

7. Seeking God. "Anyone who comes to him must believe that he exists and that he rewards those who earnestly seek him" (Hebrews 11:6). Though we don't know how Enoch sought God, we know that he did. As much as God found him, he also found God. Only those who seek the Lord with all their heart find Him, according to His Word: "You will seek Me and find Me, when you search for Me with all your heart" (Jeremiah 29:13 NKJV).

8. Focused on what is eternal. Enoch put his priorities in order. He wasn't limited by what was around him, but concentrated on what was unseen. "We do not look at the things which are seen, but at the things which are not seen. For the things which are seen are temporary, but the things which are not seen are eternal" (2 Corinthians 4:18 NKJV). The mark of greatness is the ability to see what is far as if it is near and now. What we believe shapes our value system, providing a base for our mindset to see with an open mind, as Paul prayed for the saints in Ephesus:

I keep asking that the God of our Lord Jesus Christ, the glorious
Father, may give you the Spirit of wisdom and revelation, so that you
may know him better. I pray also that the eyes of your heart may be
enlightened in order that you may know the hope to which he has
called you, the riches of his glorious inheritance in his holy people,
and his incomparably great power for us who believe.

Ephesians 1:17–19

9. Lived with God. God is looking for those who live with Him
before they try to live for Him. Enoch was the first person who
made this truth a reality. He came to walk and dwell in the presence of his God. The call of God in every generation is to come
and dwell in His presence. When Jesus called His disciples, He
illustrated this eternal truth: "Jesus went up on a mountainside
and called *to him those he wanted,* and *they came to him*" (Mark
3:13, emphasis added).

10. Was taken by God. Enoch was overtaken by the overwhelm-
ing glory, majesty, holiness, favor, and grace of God. He was sub-
merged in God's presence. The apostle John describes this reality:
"When I saw him, I fell at his feet as though dead. Then he placed
his right hand on me" (Revelation 1:17). This was John, who walked
with Jesus for more than three years and saw His glory on the Mount
of Transfiguration. This time, he was drawn to the majesty of the
King of glory and became like a dead man. That's the invitation
for everyone who would like to walk with a pure heart, clean conscience, and sincere faith. "Whoever serves me must follow me;
and where I am, my servant also will be. My Father will honor the
one who serves me" (John 12:26).

11. Was not found. "Then he was no more, because God took
him away" (Genesis 5:24). Enoch was not found for anything else,
except for God. It is the greatest accomplishment when we refuse to
be found by anything or anyone, except for God's will and purpose.

It means giving up what looks important for the time being, just as Paul did:

> But whatever was to my profit I now consider loss for the sake of Christ. What is more, I consider everything a loss compared to the surpassing greatness of knowing Christ Jesus my Lord, for whose sake I have lost all things. I consider them rubbish, that I may gain Christ.
>
> Philippians 3:7–8 NIV1984

When people make that type of dedication, they die to self, and their lives are hidden in Christ. No one and nothing will find that person, as Paul so beautifully and powerfully stated: "For I am convinced that neither death nor life, neither angels nor demons, neither the present nor the future, nor any powers, neither height nor depth, nor anything else in all creation, will be able to separate us from the love of God that is in Christ Jesus our Lord" (Romans 8:38–39).

12. *Fulfilled his prophetic destiny.* When God names a person, He affirms His eternal plan and purpose in that person's life. This is the core of prophetic destiny: "Before I was born the LORD called me; from my mother's womb he has spoken my name" (Isaiah 49:1). Our prophetic destiny is what we are created and set apart for in this life. The greatest ministry is living and dying for our preplanned purpose and will of God on earth. Jesus summarized this truth: "Now my soul is greatly distressed. And what should I say? '*Father, deliver me from this hour*'? No, but for this very reason I have come to this hour. Father, glorify your name" (John 12:27–28 NET, emphasis added). It was His unwavering commitment to glorify the Father by paying the necessary cost for His prophetic destiny. The Father responded by displaying His glory so others could see and hear His approval publicly: "Then a voice came from heaven, 'I have glorified it, and I will glorify it again'" (verse 28 NET).

The Longing of the Father's Heart

God is looking for a son or daughter and a friend before anything else. This is the reason why the Father declared aloud from heaven about Jesus, the second Adam, the Word who became flesh, "This is my Son, whom I love; with him I am well pleased" (Matthew 3:17). The Father established the right priority by saying "my Son." What pleased the Father was to find a son. It is all about relationship with God. A father's heart always longs for fellowship with sons and daughters.

As a child, I witnessed this between my father and me. I grew up in the countryside of Ethiopia, on a small farm. I was the tenth and last child. I still remember that after we put the animals into their barn, my father used to ask me to sit with him outside, on a grassy place, to talk and to ask me for advice. When I look back, I realize that he wasn't very interested in my advice, as much as he was in fellowshiping with his youngest son.

We see a similar situation between the prodigal son and his father. The father wasn't concerned or anxious about the money his son had wasted; he was longing to have his son back again for a renewed relationship. It's the same with our heavenly Father. He has been looking for individuals in every generation who will walk with Him as a friend. That's the heart of our heavenly Father!

QUESTIONS FOR ABIDING DEEPER

- Did you know that God desires a family? Is that truth a surprise to you?
- Which of Enoch's qualities are you walking in? Which would you like to grow in?
- What does your name mean, and how have you seen the prophetic significance of that in your life?

3

RECEIVING HIS FAVOR

ALEMU BEEFTU

Greetings, you who are highly favored! The Lord is with you.

Luke 1:28

God is looking for a person who would restore the reflection of His glory with total obedience. Such a person will walk in His favor. After Enoch, the second person the Lord found was Noah. For me, these two individuals paint the best picture of what God is looking for, and why—first, true fellowship, and second, a faithful messenger who reveals God's will and purpose for a generation. That is what serving God's purpose in one's generation is all about. God saw Noah and bestowed His favor upon him to be a witness among his evil generation. I can't image how much that generation grieved the Lord. However, He was very pleased to find the one person He was looking for: "But Noah found favor in the eyes of the LORD" (Genesis 6:8).

Why had Noah found favor in the Lord's eyes in his generation? The reasons for both Noah and Enoch were similar. They were walking with God, despite their surroundings. While Enoch was taken by God to be with Him, Noah found special favor to be used by God to save humanity and to bring much-needed restoration and reformation. This shows God's desire to fellowship with us and make us His messengers to reach out to our generation.

God's approval results in divine authority to fulfill His will on earth. We see this when Father God spoke about His Son: "This is my Son, whom I love; with him I am well pleased. Listen to him!" (Matthew 17:5). The command of the Father was "Listen to him!" Jesus was given full authority because of their relationship.

We observe a very similar pattern in the disciples' call. First, Jesus called them to Himself so they could be with Him. Relationship and fellowship come by being in His presence. Then He sent them out with authority and power for the work of the Kingdom: "He appointed twelve—designating them apostles—that they might be with him and that he might send them out to preach" (Mark 3:14 NIV1984). Approval of relationship results in full spiritual authority.

In a corrupted and evil generation God found Noah, who walked with Him for about 120 years while building the Ark. The mark of his life was to walk in the favor of the Lord in obedience, faith, and holy reverence for God, in spite of his challenging situation. That was what made him a man of right standing with God. God summarized his life by saying, "This is the account of Noah and his family. Noah was a righteous man, blameless among the people of his time, and he walked faithfully with God" (Genesis 6:9). Wow, what a description of character integrity—righteous, blameless, full of faith and the fear of God, walking with God.

This list wasn't about Noah's talents or gifts, however, but about the virtues that empowered him to rescue humanity from total extinction. God is continuing to look for the Noahs of today, to reach out to this generation and the nations of the world with compassion and the Gospel. The only difference is that we are not called to build an Ark, but to call our generation to the true Ark of salvation. Jesus said, "All those the Father gives Me will come to Me, and whoever comes to Me I will never drive away" (John 6:37).

The starting point is not ministry, business, or a profession. The starting point is walking with God in true humility and total obedience to His revealed will, with a pure motive and sincere faith. This will bring us close to God to hear His heart for our generation, cities, regions, nations, and world.

One night, I had a vivid dream about a pastor I had ordained in a closed nation in the Middle East. In my dream, I saw this pastor sick and lying down on the grass under a small tree. It looked as if he was fainting out of exhaustion. I came close and knelt with another pastor, and we started praying for this pastor. Something happened immediately. He got up and started flying with wings in the air, shouting, "My city, my city!"

After that dream, I found out that the exhausted pastor in it was ready to give up on his calling because of all the challenges. After I shared that dream with him, I felt things start to change. The pastor decided to continue with the calling to reach his city with a renewed vision and the power of the Holy Spirit.

One of the challenges we face as committed individuals desiring to be used by God is the temptation to depend on our talents or gifts to do God's work. But just like the pastor the Lord showed me in my dream, we get exhausted and are tempted to give up altogether, since we can't move the mountain of opposition by our own power or might. Even with all his personal experiences and calling, Zerubbabel, governor of Judea while the Temple was being rebuilt after the Babylonian exile, was unable to move the opposition. He received relief when the Lord sent an angel with a simple message to remind him of the source of his power: "'Not by might nor by power, but by my Spirit,' says the LORD Almighty" (Zechariah 4:6).

Stop depending on what you think. You must work and trust God. When we realize this, we feel as if we're flying with the wings of an eagle because of God's eternal promise: "The one who calls you is faithful, and he will do it" (1 Thessalonians 5:24). Our true calling is walking with Him in His favor, trusting in His faithfulness.

Becoming a Messenger of Rest

God's desire is to find not only a true friend, but also a faithful messenger. "Then I heard the voice of the Lord saying, 'Whom shall I send? And who will go for us?'" (Isaiah 6:8). What the prophet Isaiah heard and saw in his personal encounter in the Lord's presence made him respond, "Here am I. Send me!" Divine encounters prepare us to be God's messengers and the carriers of His holiness. That's why the Lord calls us into a relationship before He sends us into a ministry—to transform our lives and character to reflect His glory.

It is not only about our message, but about our lives. Being in the presence of the Lord changes our view of ministry, just as it did Isaiah's view. Our daily life becomes a ministry. For years, I have asked leaders to write the following during leadership workshops:

- My life is a ministry.
- My ministry is life.
- My life is a message.
- My message is life.

In relationship, true ministry is total obedience to the revealed will of God. As we reflect the glory of Jesus, we are transformed into His image. The results of a deep relationship with Him are proven character and a life of integrity. Our life and message can't be separated; one reinforces the other. However, without a true relationship with God, how can we be His messengers and reveal His heart, mind, power, and eternal will? That's why the Lord is seeking those whose hearts are fully committed to Him, since the goal of transforming ministry is to reveal God's heart.

Ministry is not what we do for God. It is our daily commitment to listen to His heart and let Him be in us and through us exactly who He is: Creator, Redeemer, Deliverer, Comforter, Protector, Provider, etc. During my morning prayer time, my little son used to come and stretch out his hands, wanting me to pick him up. I would pick him up, walk, and pray. Usually, he leaned on my chest until I finished my praying. One day, he said, "Ababa [Daddy], hush!" He was so intense that I stopped praying aloud and prayed silently. After a while, he said, "Ababa, now you can pray out loud."

I asked him, "Why did you ask me to hush?"

He said, "Because I was trying to listen to your heart, and when you prayed out loud, I was not able to hear your heart."

Since that day, my focus has been to hush, to listen to God's heart for my generation. That same boy, now 28 years old, gave me a special gift for Christmas. He told me this Christmas gift had a prophetic message. When I opened it, it was a sobering gift, a simple but life-changing message for me. It was a stethoscope. I like this definition of *stethoscope*: "a medical instrument for listening to the action of someone's heart or breathing, typically having a small, disk-shaped resonator that is placed against the chest, and two tubes connected to earpieces."[1] Since receiving that gift, my focus has been listening to the heart of my heavenly Father.

Yes, God is faithful to those who are determined to listen to His heart for their generation. That's why the Lord came to Noah with His favor, so that Noah would have the confidence to walk with Him by faith and hear His voice. On Noah's journey, what pleased the Lord more than Noah building the Ark was his willingness to listen to God's voice and obey by faith, since it is impossible to please God without faith.

God is looking at every generation to find those with a heart after Him, both for a relationship and to fulfill His will among the people of the world. Those who are walking with God and serving His purpose ought to focus on what He is looking for: a pure heart. When God finds a person after His heart, He anoints him or her, regardless of the person's qualifications. King David has been and always will be a classic example of this. God said three things about David:

1. "I have found David son of Jesse, a man after my own heart" (Acts 13:22). The Lord made an announcement to all of humanity that He had found what He was looking for.

2. "I have found David my servant; with my sacred oil I have anointed him" (Psalm 89:20). This was a kingly prophet and worshiper anointing that would remain forever. That was the reason why Jesus was called the Son of David. Just like David, Jesus was anointed by the Father: "God anointed Jesus of Nazareth with the Holy Spirit and power" (Acts 10:38). Jesus sealed this eternal truth at the beginning of His earthly ministry by reading what was written about Him by the prophet Isaiah: "The Spirit of the Lord is on me, because he has anointed me" (Luke 4:18).

3. "I have found David . . . he will do everything I want him to do" (Acts 13:22). David became a true messenger of God, doing everything according to God's plan and purpose. This is the result of walking with God, as it was in Noah's life.

A commitment to walk with God releases the favor to achieve for Him, by His grace, that which otherwise is unimaginable. Noah was known for receiving God's favor. Favor is a foundation for becoming a true messenger of the Lord, even in difficult places and circumstances.

When the angel of the Lord came to Mary, he told her that she was highly favored, full of grace, and that the Lord was with her (see Luke 1). It was a loaded and unusual greeting. The combination of favor, grace, and God's presence resulted in a virgin giving birth to the Son of God.

Noah continued his journey with God of obedience by faith because of the favor of God on his life. Because of favor and relationship, he became the first person in human history to receive a blueprint or a pattern from the Lord. His blueprint detailed how to build an Ark to save not only his family, but also both humanity and all the animal species. (The second person was Moses, when he received a blueprint to build the Tabernacle.)

Noah was named before he was born. His father understood his prophetic destiny and named him Noah, meaning *rest*, and declared, "He will comfort us in the labor and painful toil of our hands caused by the ground the LORD has cursed" (Genesis 5:29). Noah was born to bring hope and restoration by breaking the curse that had entered humanity, the curse that occurred the day Adam rebelled against God and ate the forbidden fruit: "Cursed is the ground because of you; through painful toil you will eat food from it all the days of your life" (Genesis 3:17).

Noah brought hope again by obediently walking with God, bringing rest to earth through his covenant relationship with Him. The Ark symbolized overcoming the curse of sin and destruction. While he was building the Ark, Noah became the Lord's messenger to his generation. During the flood stage, the Ark rested on Mount Ararat. *Ararat* means "the curse reversed." Noah was used by God as His messenger to bring rest by reversing the curse.

Heralds of Righteousness

When God finds people who are willing to walk with Him by faith, He uses them to reach their generation as heralds of His righteousness. Friendship and a walk of faith with our heavenly Father result in an eternal impact on present and future generations. Likewise, our friendship and walk affirm an unbreakable covenant with God. After Noah walked with the Lord as a preacher of righteousness and the curse was reversed, God accepted Noah's sacrifice of true worship. A true walk with God results in sincere and God-honoring worship. The first thing Noah did after he came out of the Ark was build an altar to God.

As true messengers of God to our generation, the altar of worship ought to be the central issue for us. God's nature requires that we worship in truth and in Spirit. Whatever we do for God or in the name of God can't replace pure worship and praise. We can only enter His gates, the presence of the King of kings, with thanksgiving. A lasting relationship with God that's based on God-honoring worship reinforces a lasting covenant that impacts many generations. That was the reason why Noah built the altar to the Lord after the Great Flood, before he did anything else. Here is the result:

> The LORD smelled the pleasing aroma and said in his heart: "Never again will I curse the ground because of humans, even though every inclination of the human heart is evil from childhood. And never again will I destroy all living creatures, as I have done.
> "As long as the earth endures, seedtime and harvest, cold and heat, summer and winter, day and night will never cease."
>
> Genesis 8:21–22

What an amazing covenant the Lord made. We receive and enjoy the fruit of that covenant even today, because of the walk of one person with God. Noah offered a sacrifice, and the Lord established an everlasting covenant that impacted all creation for eternity. The covenant God made with Noah was to bring rest and hope to earth and restore blessings after the destruction. The Lord gave earth and all humanity a second chance because of Noah's faithful obedience.

The covenant prevented worldwide destruction by another flood, promised the changing of seasons, day and night, and the restoration of the blessings from Genesis 1. "Then God blessed Noah and his sons, saying to them, 'Be fruitful and increase in number and fill the earth'" (Genesis 9:1).

QUESTIONS FOR ABIDING DEEPER

- What does it mean to you to rest before God in worship? How do you hear His heart?
- Does the concept that God desires relationship above performance surprise you? Do you feel more inclined to serve Him in relationship, or to engage in activities?
- Has God ever required radical obedience from you, as He did from Noah? What was that journey like?

4

BECOMING A COVENANT FRIEND

ALEMU BEEFTU

But you, Israel, my servant, Jacob, whom I have chosen, you descendants of Abraham my friend . . .

Isaiah 41:8

After Noah's death, his descendants did not obey the Lord. Unlike their faithful father, they did not build an altar as a symbol of obedience and worship to God. Instead, they built a city in their own name. As they started building, the Lord was watching: "The LORD came down to see the city and the tower the people were building" (Genesis 11:5). Noah received the blueprint to build the Ark, but his descendants didn't ask the Lord for a blueprint. They were building so their own name could reach heaven, not to reach future generations. The Lord saw what Noah had built, approved it, and used it. But when God saw what Noah's descendants were building, He confused their language and scattered them throughout the world. Now, that generation was not only without a message of righteousness, but also without hope and direction.

However, God did not give up on the salvation of human beings. From this scattered group, God chose someone from the family of Terah with whom He could establish an everlasting covenant. God needed a person who would combine the life of Enoch (walking with God as a worshiper and companion) and Noah (a righteous messenger of salvation). So God began to look for another friend who would walk with Him and receive His everlasting covenant for the salvation of humankind, and He found one, Abram. He called Abram to walk with Him, to be His friend, and to father a generation. Covenant became the only hope for salvation, reconciliation, restoration, redemption, lasting relationship, and victory over sin and iniquities. The central message of the Bible became about covenant. The Old Testament is about a covenant of hope, while the New Testament is the fulfillment of that covenant through Jesus.

To enter a covenant relationship, God called Abram out from where he was and brought him to where he should be. Then Abram could walk with God as a friend and be the messenger of hope. Abram became not only the father of faith, but also the father of many nations. Abram's call into a lasting covenant included his willingness to accept God's call, leave the past for a new covenant, and have vision for the new. Let's look at each of these more closely.

A Willingness to Accept God's Call

The most important call in human history was the call of Abram into a covenant relationship with God. His call began when he stepped forward from where he was to where he was meant to be. By accepting God's call and starting a new journey, he completed the journey his forefather, Terah, had started, and he went beyond it for the sake of future generations. Terah had set out to reach the land of Canaan, but instead of reaching his destination, he had stopped, settled, and lived in Haran for ten years.

Terah, whose name means "delay" or "wandering," died without completing the journey or reaching the destination. He understood the importance of going to Canaan, but missed the open door for ten years. He failed to maximize the opportunity God gave him. Obedience is therefore better than sacrifice. Stepping toward your calling involves passion and vision. Completing the calling is a test of character and faith. As powerful as passion might be, it cannot be sustained without commitment or character as you endure challenges on the journey. Passion without character is like fire without firewood.

The call of God begins by setting people free from their past to prepare them for what is coming. Accepting the call means letting go of your past with an anticipation for a new thing. This also means coming out of an old mindset and allowing your mind and values to be renewed. The foundation of true, lasting values is your belief system. What we believe is the foundation for our actions and allows us to accept God's calling. Our beliefs also allow us to receive new guidance.

By releasing the past, you have confidence to envision the future. This is the reason why accepting your calling means accepting and knowing your true identity. Once a person knows who he or she is, a lifelong journey of living for a clearer purpose begins.

Moses also left behind his past to focus on the future of his calling. Because he accepted his calling and was focused on his future, when the time came to leave Egypt by faith, he didn't hesitate. For forty years, he lived in the wilderness, in submission to God's will. When it was time, he went back to Egypt to deliver the people of God. "He regarded disgrace for the sake of Christ as of greater value than the treasures of Egypt, because he was looking ahead to his reward" (Hebrews 11:26).

Accepting the call of God to walk in divine approval and authority, and affirming our identity, means living a life of covenant relationship with our Creator and Redeemer. We become a channel of His blessings to others, as we work with Him in a covenant relationship, just like Abram.

Leaving the Past for a New Covenant

To pursue the call of God and enter a lasting covenant relationship means leaving everything in the past. In Abram's case, he left his country, his people, and his family's household as a sign of a new beginning for a new covenant. Paul stated, "But one thing I do: Forgetting what is behind and straining toward what is ahead" (Philippians 3:13). It doesn't matter how big or small the thing you are leaving might be; it's the willingness to leave it behind that matters.

After I completed ninth grade, the Lord called me to go to Bible school and prepare myself for full-time ministry. I fought against this. When I told my parents that I had applied to go to Bible school, my father was furious. All my friends were dismayed at my decision to take entry tests for Bible school. They thought I was losing my mind! One of my teachers thought I was quitting school because of financial problems and offered to cover all my expenses. I had to say, "No, thank you."

At the end of the summer, I didn't have money for clothes, transportation, school tuition, and all the other necessary things to start Bible school. I was leaving to take the entrance exam on a Tuesday, but I didn't have money. The Sunday before, I went to my small country church to give a testimony about my call to Bible school and say good-bye to the congregation. The offering time came before I was invited to the pulpit. The only thing I had was 25 cents, and I heard the Holy Spirit say to give it as an offering. I struggled. I didn't want to give those 25 cents; it was literally all I had! Finally, I relented to the Spirit and threw it into the offering.

Then I gave my testimony and shared about my calling to Bible school. After the service, a missionary kid about my age came to say good-bye and handed me an envelope full of money. He said he had worked for his parents all summer and had earned this money, but that morning, the Lord told him to give it to me . . . all of it.

I asked him, "Are you sure?"

He answered with joy on his face, "I am very sure. Have a blessed journey to Bible school."

The next day, I bought some clothes, got a haircut, and purchased a bus ticket. I arrived at Grace Bible School and was greeted by the school director. The next day, he called me into his office. After welcoming me to school, he said, "The other good news for you is that somebody came this week and paid your tuition for three years."

That day, I embraced my calling and understood that the way to fulfill our prophetic destiny is by surrendering and giving up the old to receive the new. The journey of a new covenant begins when you leave behind the past to go forward. When the Lord told Abram to leave his country, his people, and his father's household, He was asking him to leave his homeland for a new country, prepared for his descendants, that would flow with milk and honey. God asked Abram to exchange Teran for Canaan as a covenant sign. Abram also had to leave behind people from his past to receive a new generation that would outnumber the sands of the sea. By leaving his father's house and following God for the new covenant, Abram became Abraham. God told him, "As for me, this is my covenant with you: You will be the father of many nations. No longer will you be called Abram; your name will be Abraham, for I have made you a father of many nations" (Genesis 17:4–5).

Having Vision for the New

The foundation for a new covenant is someone's willingness to leave behind his or her past season, authority, and relationships. That's how covenant starts between a husband and wife: "For this reason a man shall leave his father and his mother, and shall be joined to his wife; and they shall become one flesh" (Genesis 2:24 AMP). That unity provides strength and direction for the journey of covenant.

Abraham's covenant relationship was based on a future vision. The Lord told him, "Go from your country, your people and your father's household to the land I will show you" (Genesis 12:1). Abraham's willingness to follow God's lead and go to a new land showed submission to God's plan. Since he didn't know the place he was going to, it was a journey of faith. From that initial journey, Abraham lived and walked with God by faith all his life, and it was credited to him as righteousness.

Faith is believing and standing on God's promises, and our lifestyle is shaped by what we believe. Abraham's journey of faith was part of a lasting covenant that would become the hope of future generations. Abraham accepted not only land, but also future descendants by believing the word of the Lord, who said He would make Abraham into a great nation. As Isaiah says,

> Listen to me, you who pursue righteousness and who seek the LORD: Look to the rock from which you were cut and to the quarry from which you were hewn; look to Abraham, your father, and to Sarah, who gave you birth. When I called him he was only one man, and I blessed him and made him many.
>
> Isaiah 51:1–2

Abraham not only followed the Lord to receive land and descendants, but also because he sought righteousness. He left everything behind to receive these blessings, which would be for all humanity: "All peoples on earth will be blessed through you" (Genesis 12:3). He obediently followed God into the Promised Land, and along this journey of faith, the Lord entered an eternal, unbreakable covenant for the salvation of humanity. That covenant was completed through the death and resurrection of the Lord Jesus Christ.

God fulfilled the promise of making Abraham's name great by changing his name from Abram to Abraham, meaning "father of a multitude." He also affirmed His covenant with Abraham's descendants through the act of circumcision. God used these signs to signify that Abraham had become a father of faith and a friend of God: "And the scripture was fulfilled that says, 'Abraham believed God, and it was credited to him as righteousness,' and he was called God's friend" (James 2:23; see also 2 Chronicles 20:7).

God's covenant with Abraham is fully realized in Jesus, the true messenger of God, who gave His life and became the final messenger of salvation:

> Christ redeemed us from the curse of the law by becoming a curse for us, for it is written: "Cursed is everyone who is hung on a tree." He redeemed us in order that the blessing given to Abraham might come to the Gentiles through Christ Jesus, so that by faith we might receive the promise of the Spirit.
>
> Galatians 3:13–14 NIV1984

In Jesus, God demonstrated the friendship, salvation, and lasting covenant He desired, and as the messenger of God, Jesus revealed the Father. "For the law was given through Moses; grace and truth came through Jesus Christ. No one has ever seen God, but the one and only Son, who is himself God and is in closest relationship with the Father, has made him known" (John 1:17–18).

God seeks someone in every generation who is willing to be set apart. He seeks a person willing to walk with Him, receive His favor, experience the message of salvation, and walk in a covenant relationship to share the hope of redemption with the world. God desires our fellowship with Him more than our activities for Him; our sonship is more important than our sacrifice. Just as Enoch walked in friendship with God, God is looking for you in this generation—not for what you can accomplish for Him, but so that you can walk with Him as His son or daughter.

Once you start a close walk with Him, there is no turning back. Are you willing to be in His presence? Can you say today as a child of God, "I can't be for anything else; I just want His will"? That's the call. That's why Jesus called the disciples to Himself. In God's presence we receive favor, grace, and anointing to fulfill His will on earth. After the resurrection, during Jesus' first appearance to the apostles, He gave them the mandate of the New Testament calling: *Receive the Holy Spirit and allow yourself to be sent.* "Again Jesus said, 'Peace be with you! As the Father has sent me, I am sending you'" (John 20:21).

Jesus revealed the ministry model. The power is provided by the Holy Spirit, the authority has been established in Jesus, and He is the one who sends us out. Ministry is not going and doing; it is existing to be sent by the One who has all authority both in heaven and on earth. It is important to remember that God doesn't call us to ministry, but to Himself, so we can be sent to do His will and impact our generation.

When we look at Enoch, Noah, and Abraham, we see the three dimensions of effective ministry that the Lord is looking for today in our generation:

- *Enoch:* He walked with God. He was not found for anything else except to do God's will, and he was hidden in the presence of God.
- *Noah:* He walked in the favor of God and brought true restoration on earth. We are also mandated to bring reformation and transformation to our communities, neighborhoods, cities, states, and nations by breaking the curse of sin by the power of the Gospel.

- *Abraham:* He walked by faith as a friend of God and became the carrier of God's presence and glory. He became a channel of God's blessings to others through the unbreakable covenant he had with God. A lasting covenant requires building and protecting the altar of worship to God: "So he built an altar there to the LORD, who had appeared to him" (Genesis 12:7). Covenant relationship brings us into a revelation of God's presence.

God is looking to walk with you, put His favor on your life, affirm His covenant, make you His own, and send you to impact your generation by serving His purpose and redeeming the times. The Lord has need of you. Let's respond to His call the way David did: "When You said, 'Seek My face,' my heart said to You, 'Your face, LORD, I will seek'" (Psalm 27:8 NKJV). Let's start the journey with God today by seeking His face.

QUESTIONS FOR ABIDING DEEPER

- What are the mindsets that you need to cast off so you can believe and step into the new things God has for you?
- What are some things God is asking you to leave behind?
- How do you feel about the idea of being set apart from your generation, for the redemption of your generation?

5

DWELLING IN THE GLORY ZONE

ALEMU BEEFTU

Moses entered the cloud as he went on up the mountain. And he stayed on the mountain forty days and forty nights.

Exodus 24:18

After Noah, God chose Abraham and established a covenant relationship by moving Abraham from where he was to where he ought to be, revealing to him the Promised Land. Abraham worshiped the Lord by building an altar, securing the inheritance and the presence of God. In that covenant, God promised to bless him and make him a blessing to the nations.

This friendship was based on the plan and purpose of God, and Abraham's willingness to walk faithfully with Him. From the first time God called Abraham until the day he bound his son Isaac on the altar, Abraham faithfully obeyed. This relationship pleased God, so He promised that after four hundred years, He would rescue

Abraham's descendants from their oppressors and bring them back to the Promised Land.

When God finds His people in the right place at the right time, He accomplishes His purpose. The right time and right place are the most important ingredients for fulfilling the promises of God. That's what makes abiding in His presence so important.

As promised, the Lord delivered Abraham's descendants from Pharaoh and brought them out from Egypt to the Promised Land. During their deliverance from Egypt, they experienced the power of God. Now the time came for them to know Him not only as a deliverer, but also as their God and Father. The "I Am" sought to dwell among them as their Good Shepherd, to guide, protect, and provide for them (see Psalm 23). He wanted them to experience His presence through true worship. That's why the meeting tent was needed, so God instructed Moses, "Then have them make a sanctuary for me, and I will dwell among them. Make this tabernacle and all its furnishings exactly like the pattern I will show you" (Exodus 25:8–9).

The Lord appointed Moses not only to bring deliverance, but also to make a sanctuary while the Israelites were still in the wilderness. For God to come and dwell among them, He needed a place as a point of connection, a place that would welcome the manifestation of His presence. God desires for us to keep our passion for Him alive by dwelling in His presence and beholding His glory.

Recently, I spoke to Christian leaders at a conference in Indonesia on the topic of leaders keeping their passion for the Lord alive. I told them if we are committed to starting and finishing with passion for the Lord, we ought to refocus on the Lord, not on our ministry or leadership goals and purposes. Purpose is very helpful for leaders carrying out an agenda for measurable success or outcomes. However, leaders who are serious about keeping their passion ought to replace success with impact, and a purpose-driven leadership style with Jesus Christ.

Passion is the result of a relationship. A leader who is driven by the beauty and majesty of God draws closer to Him daily to dwell in the glory zone, as Moses did. It isn't about how many years a leader has waited for the Lord or how successful a person has been.

The Lord called Moses from the fire. That fire of vision, the manifested presence of God, changed that physical place and Moses' soul. The dry wasteland suddenly became holy ground where Moses couldn't walk with his shoes on because of the presence of God. "'Do not come any closer,' God said. 'Take off your sandals, for the place where you are standing is holy ground'" (Exodus 3:5). Moses took off his shoes and covered his face in reverence. The manifested presence of the Lord changes not only individuals, but also the atmosphere. That's the reason why we call it *the glory zone*.

The impact of dwelling in the glory zone goes beyond renewing a personal passion for God. It isn't just a fiery start and finish to your life. Dwelling in the glory zone also helps us receive divine designs to build what can host God's glory, His message, His grace, and His Word to impact the next generation. It transforms us and develops a greater hunger for Him and His glory.

Personal Transformation

Moses was invited into the presence of God to dwell in the glory zone. "The LORD descended to the top of Mount Sinai and called Moses to the top of the mountain. So Moses went up" (Exodus 19:20). Going up to where the cloud of God's glory covered the mountain gave Moses a deeper understanding of God's holiness. It prepared him to continue his walk with the Lord with greater humility and an unquenchable thirst for the greater glory. The process of personal transformation begins in the glory zone on the mountain of God.

God's plan is to change us into His image so that we would reflect His glory and abide in His presence. The call of God is "Come up here," not for what we can do for Him, but for what He would like to do in us. "For those God foreknew he also predestined to be conformed to the image of his Son, that he might be the firstborn among many brothers" (Romans 8:29). On the mountain of God, we don't see anything else except His glory. We only hear His voice. His presence transforms us into His image. When Moses came down the mountain, "his face was radiant because he had spoken with the LORD" (Exodus 34:29).

Moses didn't know, however, that others could see the inner transformation on his face. Ministry, leadership, or a purpose-driven lifestyle can't produce such a glorious change. Only a Christ-driven life of abiding in God's presence can renew our passion for Him and make us more like Him. Everything we do for God is very good, but it can't change us into His image, and it won't increase our passion for Him.

That's one of the reasons why the apostle Paul encouraged believers to turn to the Lord Jesus and walk in the freedom of the Holy Spirit if they wanted to be transformed into His likeness. The Lord Jesus' job, according to John the Baptizer, was "He will baptize you with the Holy Spirit and fire" (Matthew 3:11). The Holy Spirit ignites our passion for the Lord and turns us toward Him. "And we, who with unveiled faces all reflect the Lord's glory, are being transformed into his likeness with ever-increasing glory, which comes from the Lord, who is the Spirit" (2 Corinthians 3:18 NIV1984).

Greater Hunger for the Glory

Once you dwell in the glory zone, a spiritual appetite forms in you, and your desires change. Moses started his assignment with a divine encounter at the burning bush. After that, he walked in signs and wonders. He dwelt in the presence of God. "The LORD would speak to Moses face to face, as one speaks to a friend" (Exodus 33:11). Such a relationship increased his reverence for God, and he warned the people to fear God: "For the LORD your God is a consuming fire, a jealous God" (Deuteronomy 4:24).

Moses walked in total humility before God: "Now Moses was a very humble man, more humble than anyone else on the face of the earth" (Numbers 12:3). His great desire was to walk in the favor of the Lord until the end. He told God, "If you are pleased with me, teach me your ways so I may know you and continue to find favor with you. Remember that this nation is your people" (Exodus 33:13).

Moses didn't want to lead the people without the manifested presence of God. He wanted the presence of the Lord to be both his identity and the nation's identity: "How will anyone know that you are pleased with me and with your people unless you go with us? What else will distinguish me and your people from all the other people on the face of the earth?" (Exodus 33:16).

Finally, Moses had an ever-increasing hunger and passion for the glory of the Lord. He was both carrying and reflecting the glory and presence of God with him. His prayer was not for his success, but to see more of the glory of God: "Then Moses said, 'Now show me Your glory'" (Exodus 33:18).

Yes, dwelling in God's presence creates a greater hunger in us for God's glory, and it ignites our passion for the Lord.

Receiving Revelation of God's Word

Moses went to the mountain to receive God's message for His people, and to hear God's word and be in His presence under the dense glory cloud. He stayed on the mountain for forty days and nights without eating or drinking. That's dwelling in the glory zone in a place of revelation, as well as abiding in His presence! That was why God called Moses to come higher. "Then Moses went up to God, and the LORD called to him from the mountain and said, 'This is what you are to say to the descendants of Jacob and what you are to tell the people of Israel'" (Exodus 19:3).

Moses received a timely message for the people by dwelling in God's presence. "Moses alone is to approach the LORD; the others must not come near. And the people may not come up with him" (Exodus 24:2).

Moses was also trusted with the eternal word of God, not only in receiving it as the written Word from the Lord's hand, but also as the word to teach the people. He told them,

> He declared to you his covenant, the Ten Commandments, which he commanded you to follow and then wrote them on two stone tablets. And the LORD directed me at that time to teach you the decrees and laws you are to follow in the land that you are crossing the Jordan to possess.
>
> Deuteronomy 4:13–14

Receiving a Pattern for Building

God also gave Moses a pattern on the mountain for building His Tabernacle, the glory zone. God created the original design for the Tabernacle to fully express His desire to continue the friendship He had established with Abraham. After Abraham, Moses was the one who was very close to God, speaking with Him face-to-face. He became a friend of God, just like Abraham.

Moses was "faithful as a servant in all God's house" (Hebrews 3:5). True faith and a close walk with God produce godly character and personal transformation, and they release a divine pattern. Moses experienced God's presence before he received the pattern for the Tabernacle. Relationship ought to precede assignments, commissions, or mandates from God.

When God found Moses to be a close friend and faithful servant, He revealed the Tabernacle's plans to him in detail. Having Moses build a Tabernacle fulfilled God's desire to dwell among His people because of His covenant and love for them. *God longs to be with and among His people, even more than we desire to be in His presence.* God is also looking for a friend today to whom He can release the manifestation of His presence. To receive this, Moses became a close friend of God and was faithful in His house (see Hebrews 3:2). Moses' relationship with God was about friendship, while God's faithfulness was about Moses' character.

The primary purpose of the Tabernacle was for the Lord to dwell among His people. The Tabernacle established a path for them to approach a holy God and worship Him with all their mind, soul, and strength. Through the Tabernacle, God demonstrated His standard of worship. He showed the people His manifested presence so they would be able to worship Him. Worshiping God can't be placed on the back burner. It can't wait until we arrive at our destiny or destination, and we can't hold back. The Lord didn't wait until His people came to the Promised Land to establish a system of worship for them. He showed them how to worship according to His standard while they were journeying in the wilderness.

Even those who didn't enter the Promised Land worshiped God in the desert. To worship Him in Spirit and in truth, they needed to know how to approach this holy and awesome God. By nature, God is a devouring fire; He dwells in unapproachable light and glory. Through the Tabernacle, God showed them how to enter His presence and offer sacrifices of praise without being consumed by His holiness. He taught them how to seek His face and follow the Ark of His might, power, and glory. He demonstrated how to have holy reverence for His name and glory.

The people also learned how to worship the Lord through giving burnt offerings, grain and fellowship offerings, sin offerings, guilt offerings, freewill offerings, first fruits, and tithes. They needed to learn how to worship God through giving while they were still on a journey to the Promised Land. True worship always involves giving and receiving. The Lord promised them through this process that He would release His blessings on them: "Worship the LORD your

God, and his blessing will be on your food and water. I will take away sickness from among you, and none will miscarry or be barren in your land. I will give you a full life span" (Exodus 23:25–26). Building the Tabernacle according to God's design therefore was for blessing the people as much as it was for preparing a place for the glory of God. God wanted worship to be ongoing so His presence could abide among them. He inhabits the worship and praises of His people.

The Tabernacle also provided a prophetic picture for what was coming. Just as Moses prepared the Tabernacle in order for God's glory to dwell among His people, Father God prepared Christ's body so He could tabernacle amongst us:

> Therefore, when Christ came into the world, he said: "Sacrifice and offering you did not desire, but a body you prepared for me; with burnt offerings and sin offerings you were not pleased. Then I said, 'Here I am—it is written about me in the scroll—I have come to do your will, my God.'"
>
> Hebrews 10:5–7

The price Jesus paid for our sins gave us access to entering the place of grace to worship the Lord in Spirit and truth. That's the reason why Jesus, who was full of grace and truth, came to tabernacle among us. "The Word became flesh and made his dwelling among us. We have seen his glory, the glory of the one and only Son, who came from the Father, full of grace and truth" (John 1:14). Because of this prophetic significance, God warned Moses to build the Tabernacle according to what He showed him on the mountain. Even small changes or modifications of the pattern could have affected the prophetic picture, since God's blueprint is eternal.

What God does is eternal, and it has implications for both present and future generations. The pattern that hosts His glory should be treated as holy, to be set apart for a special purpose, not common or ordinary. As such, the glory must be kept pure, not to be mixed with human plans or strategies. David summarized this process of receiving God's pattern: "'All this,' David said, 'I have in writing as a result of the LORD's hand on me, and he enabled me to understand all the details of the plan'" (1 Chronicles 28:19).

We must pay attention to receiving the right pattern, comprehending it, and implementing what comes from the Holy Spirit. For a believer, receiving a pattern is all about discerning the revealed will of God. As Acts 22:14 says, "The God of our ancestors has chosen you to know his will and to see the Righteous One and to hear words from his mouth." Studying the pattern you receive with intellectual analysis is not the point. Like David, wait upon the Lord for the Holy Spirit's revelation. The pattern is the foundational truth God gives us to build. Revelation is the leading of the Holy Spirit, step-by-step, to build according to the pattern, without adding to it or trying to modify it for culture. Faithfulness to what we receive from God qualifies us to build, for His glory, a life that accurately reflects His presence to the world.

In summary, the purpose of the divine pattern God reveals is to prepare a place for the Ark of God's presence to dwell in its fullness. God's pattern is the only option we can use. It is not a matter of opinion, but rather a command we must obey. Therefore, the call today is that we must run to God and abide in His presence until we are transformed into His likeness. We need to renew our passion for Him, receive the revelation of the Word of God, and receive His divine pattern to build what would host His glorious presence. That's the way the Spirit of God is moving. Moses stayed in the presence of God on the mountain, under the covering of the glory, until all of these took place in his life.

One of the most important things is abiding in the glory zone, waiting for God. The challenge today is that we don't have the patience to wait upon the Lord for His pattern, so we work with patterns we create under the label of short-term and long-term strategic planning goals. They appear to be very impressive, but the real questions are, *Where is the glory the Lord wants to reveal through us for the world to see? Where is the passion? Where is the hunger for the greater glory?*

QUESTIONS FOR ABIDING DEEPER

- Can you think back to a time when you received a plan or pattern from God? What was it?
- What does it look like for you to abide in God's presence, as Moses did, and dwell in the glory zone in your everyday life?

6

ANOINTING TO ABIDE IN HIS PRESENCE

ALEMU BEEFTU

You know what has happened . . . how God anointed Jesus of Nazareth with the Holy Spirit and power, and how He went around doing good and healing all who were under the power of the devil, because God was with Him.

Acts 10:37–38

The Lord promised to bless Abraham and multiply his descendants, thereby shining His glory throughout earth. The call of the Israelites has been to be a light to the Gentiles. This light reflects God's eternal glory through a covenant relationship, and that relationship comes from dwelling in His presence and worshiping Him. Abraham started his covenant journey by building an altar to the Lord: "So he built an altar there to the LORD, who had appeared to him"

(Genesis 12:7). Since then, the Lord's covenant call to Abraham's descendants has been to build an altar of worship and keep it pure for the manifested presence of God.

The presence of God demands true worship since He inhabits the praises of His people. Worship is not just a Sunday morning ritual; it is an entry point into the presence of God. It is also a way into the glory zone to receive ongoing revelation of His Word and the power of the Holy Spirit. God's truth and the power and anointing of the Holy Spirit are foundational for acceptable worship and for hosting His presence. "Yet a time is coming and has now come when the true worshipers will worship the Father in Spirit and in truth, for they are the kind of worshipers the Father seeks. God is spirit, and his worshipers must worship in the Spirit and in truth" (John 4:23–24).

Some fundamental factors to hosting God's transformative presence are recognizing the importance of His presence, understanding expressions of His presence, and having an anointing to abide in His presence. Let's examine each of these factors in closer detail.

Recognizing the Importance of His Presence

The Lord called Abraham "My" friend. Friendship is a relationship based on sincere commitment and agreement, which God expressed through the Abrahamic covenant. Abiding in God's presence requires you to recognize the importance of His presence, making it central in your daily life. The centrality of the manifested presence of God can't be replaced by anything else. The major distinction between hell and heaven is the absence of God in hell. The glory of heaven is God's presence.

By acknowledging our deepest need for God's presence, we can then cry for His presence, as Moses did: "Now show me Your glory" (Exodus 33:18). God had promised Abraham that He would deliver his children from slavery after four hundred years, bringing them back to the Promised Land and dwelling among them as their God.

Moses was that deliverer, and he experienced God's presence at the burning bush in the form of fire:

> So Moses thought, "I will go over and see this strange sight—why the bush does not burn up."
>
> When the LORD saw that he had gone over to look, God called to him from within the bush, "Moses! Moses!"
>
> And Moses said, "Here I am."
>
> "Do not come any closer," God said. "Take off your sandals, for the place where you are standing is holy ground." Then he said, "I am the God of your father, the God of Abraham, the God of Isaac and the God of Jacob." At this, Moses hid his face, because he was afraid to look at God.
>
> Exodus 3:3–6

Deliverance started through the manifestation of God's presence. There is no true freedom without the presence of God. When Moses heard God call from the fire "Moses! Moses!" he answered, "Here I am [in Your presence, for Your will and purpose]." Since God's presence requires holiness and brings transformation, the Lord told Moses to take off his shoes, representing any past life experiences. Moses took off his shoes, and because of the intensity of God's presence, he had to cover his face. Covering his face was a sign of recognizing and welcoming the presence of God with holy fear, reverence, and worship.

Here, the Lord revealed His heart for His people to Moses. Recognizing God's presence enables us to understand His loving mercy for His people. The Lord told Moses, "I have indeed seen the misery of my people in Egypt" (Exodus 3:7).

Furthermore, God's presence exposes the hidden work of the enemy, delivering lasting victory and the fulfillment of God's promises. The Lord unfolded His plan through His manifested presence as He told Moses, "I have come down" (Exodus 3:8). The purpose of His coming down was to fulfill the covenant He had made with Abraham in Genesis 15 to rescue the people from the hands of their enemies and "to bring them up out of that land into a good and spacious land, a land flowing with milk and honey" (Exodus 3:8).

The Lord confirmed Moses' calling: "I am sending you" (Exodus 3:10). You may remember that Moses had tried to set God's people free from slavery in Egypt before. The major difference was that the first time, Moses had tried it without the presence of God. He went to deliver them without being sent. This time, Moses was not willing to try it in his own power. However, the Lord gave him an unquestionable assurance of success. The first assurance was the sign of God sending him: "So now, go. I am sending you to Pharaoh to bring my people the Israelites out of Egypt" (verse 10). The second assurance was the seal of His presence: "I will be with you" (verse 12). The presence of the Lord always brings us into a place of worship and greater glory: "When you have brought the people out of Egypt, you will worship God on this mountain" (verse 12). The third assurance was the revelation of God's name: "I Am who I Am" (verse 14). Whenever Moses needed anything, "I Am" would be there with him. This is the highest sign of the presence of God.

God's presence brought new levels of authority, vision, favor, and anointing into Moses' hand. Where the presence of God is, natural things become supernatural, impossible things become possible, and insignificant things become especially important. To remove Moses' fear and doubt, the only thing "I Am" asked him was, "What is that in your hand?" (Exodus 4:2). When Moses let go of what was insignificant in his hand, it became a tool of authority to perform miracles because of "I Am."

Understanding Expressions of His Presence

To recognize and be sensitive to God's presence, it's important to understand some of the ways He expresses that presence. He revealed Himself to Moses from the burning bush. After Moses brought the people out of Egypt, the presence of God led them into freedom and the Promised Land as fire and a cloud:

> By day the LORD went ahead of them in a pillar of cloud to guide them on their way and by night in a pillar of fire to give them light, so that they could travel by day or night. Neither the pillar of cloud by day nor the pillar of fire by night left its place in front of the people.
>
> Exodus 13:21–22

For forty years, the pillar of cloud during the day and the pillar of fire at night never left them. The Lord's presence, expressed through cloud and fire, provided what they needed, including protection from the enemy. When they reached the Red Sea, the presence of God came between them and their enemy:

> The pillar of cloud also moved from in front and stood behind them, coming between the armies of Egypt and Israel. Throughout the night the cloud brought darkness to the one side and light to the other side; so neither went near the other all night long.
>
> Exodus 14:19–20

God's presence became their light in darkness and their confidence in fear and doubt.

The presence of God also welcomed them at Mount Sinai. This was the same cloud of His glorious presence that had divided the Red Sea, destroyed their enemies, and provided water and manna in the wilderness. Now, they were accepted at Mount Sinai with the cloud and fire of His glorious presence. The presence of God led them, and "I Am" carried them to the mountain where He spoke to Moses not only about their deliverance, but also about their worship. God had told him, "I will be with you. And this will be the sign to you that it is I who have sent you: When you have brought the people out of Egypt, you will worship God on this mountain" (Exodus 3:12).

The primary purpose of this people's deliverance was to worship and serve God alone. We can only experience the fullness of His presence through worship. That was the reason why He brought them out of slavery, to Himself: "I carried you on eagles' wings and brought you to myself" (Exodus 19:4). At Mount Sinai, He welcomed them with glory fire: "To the Israelites the glory of the LORD looked like a consuming fire on top of the mountain" (Exodus 24:17).

In Exodus 19, the Lord instructed the people to purify themselves for three days. After the three days of preparation, they were brought out from their tents to meet with God: "Then Moses led the people out of the camp to meet with God, and they stood at the foot of the mountain" (verse 17). They saw His manifested presence and were stunned: "On the morning of the third day there was thunder and lightning, with a thick cloud over the mountain, and a very loud trumpet blast. Everyone in the camp trembled" (verse 16). Abiding in the presence of God requires holiness and fear of the Lord, which lead to true worship. Without sincere fear and worship, we can't experience His presence. Furthermore, they heard the voice of God from the fire and cloud of His presence: "The LORD our God has shown us his glory and his majesty, and we have heard His voice from the fire" (Deuteronomy 5:24).

The three apostles Peter, James, and John had a similar experience with hearing the mighty voice of God when Jesus took them to the Mount of Transfiguration: "While he was still speaking, a bright cloud covered them, and a voice from the cloud said, 'This is my Son, whom I love; with him I am well pleased. Listen to him!'" (Matthew 17:5). After completing His earthly ministry, Jesus was taken by the same cloud of God, and He will return in the same manifested presence in a cloud of glory one day soon. That is our blessed hope.

An Anointing to Abide

After the Mount Sinai encounter, the Lord moved into a permanent presence where He would dwell amongst His people, in spite of their rebelliousness and unbelief. The Lord asked Moses to build Him a Tabernacle: "Then have them make a sanctuary for me, and I will dwell among them. Make this tabernacle and all its furnishings exactly like the pattern I will show you" (Exodus 25:8–9). In their building of the Tabernacle, the Lord highlighted that they should take the following steps: *follow the pattern, anoint the priests,* and *anoint to restore His presence.* Let's briefly explore each of these steps.

Follow the Pattern

The Lord called Moses to the mountain to be with Him for forty days and nights, to receive the pattern and build according to the blueprint he was shown. This is very important: *What ushers in the presence of God is only what is built according to His plan and for His purpose.* Moses built the Tabernacle according to the pattern, and then he "inspected the work and saw that they had done it just as the LORD had commanded. So Moses blessed them" (Exodus 39:43).

During the building process, Moses involved others by having them contribute according to their gifts and resources. The skilled workers told him, "The people are bringing more than enough for doing the work the LORD commanded to be done" (Exodus 36:5). Moses also gave other people responsibility according to their skills, anointing, and commitment to the work of God. "So Bezalel, Oholiab and every skilled person to whom the LORD has given skill and ability to know how to carry out all the work of constructing the sanctuary are to do the work just as the LORD has commanded" (Exodus 36:1).

Moses received the Tabernacle's pattern as a visionary leader, while Bezalel and Oholiab implemented the vision. Aaron and the priests managed the Tabernacle and facilitated worship, while the people provided the resources for doing the building. The Tabernacle was completed and accepted by the Lord as His dwelling place among the people.

Anoint the Priests

Anointing the high priest and other priests to serve the Lord was the second important step they needed to take. God instructed Moses to make special garments for the priests who would serve in the Tabernacle. The sacred garments for the high priest set him apart and affirmed his calling, identity, and spiritual authority to receive God's presence. The priests' anointing allowed them to stand before God and minister to Him in worship, offering sacrifices on behalf of the people, teaching them about God's instruction, and pronouncing the blessings of God upon them (see Numbers 6:23–26).

During the restoration of the Temple later, King Hezekiah admonished the priests, "My sons, do not be negligent now, for the LORD has chosen you to stand before him and serve him, to minister before him and to burn incense" (2 Chronicles 29:11). God's desire was to dwell among His people, so He needed a special place as a point of contact. Once the manifestation of His presence became a reality, the Lord wanted people to know how to abide in His presence. He chose and qualified priests, prophets, and kings in the Old Testament, anointing them to stand before Him, but the anointing was made for priests to abide in His presence. Prophets and kings were also anointed to dwell in His presence but had different roles than the priests.

In the New Testament, all believers are anointed and called priests, and all are capable of abiding in God's presence. This is also the core of our salvation: "To him who loves us and has freed us from our sins by his blood, and has made us to be a kingdom and priests to serve his God and Father—to him be glory and power for ever and ever! Amen" (Revelation 1:5–6).

Moses built the Tabernacle according to the pattern God showed him, and he prepared and anointed the priests. "Their anointing will be to a priesthood that will continue for all generations to come" (Exodus 40:15 NIV1984). He raised the Tabernacle as a place to host God's presence. "Then the cloud covered the tent of meeting, and the glory of the LORD filled the tabernacle" (Exodus 40:34). The Israelites witnessed the same thing at the completion of King Solomon's Temple, built according to the pattern King David received in writing from the hand of God: "When the priests withdrew from the Holy Place, the cloud filled the temple of the LORD" (1 Kings 8:10). That means God's presence had come to dwell with His people!

God gave the priests the responsibility of abiding in His presence through worship and protecting the altar fire: "The fire must be kept burning on the altar continuously; it must not go out" (Leviticus 6:13). Without the fire of worship, holiness, love, and dedication, the Lord's presence cannot be maintained.

In my view, the major sin in the Old Testament was letting the fire of the altar go out because of the sin and negligence of the priests. We see this happen with the sons of Eli, the high priest, as they defiled the altar of the Lord. They dishonored His altar by snatching the sacrifices and keeping them for themselves (see 1 Samuel 2). This resulted in God's glory departing from the nation. The sons of Eli were killed in a battle, and the Ark of the Lord was captured. From that time on, the Israelites were without the Ark of His presence.

Anoint to Restore His Presence

God started to look for a person who would restore His presence to the nation of Israel for years to come. Because of the sins of Eli and his sons, God was looking for a faithful person who would restore and dwell in His presence. The Lord said, "I will raise up for myself a faithful priest, who will do according to what is in my heart and mind. I will firmly establish his house, and he will minister before my anointed one always" (1 Samuel 2:35).

The Lord says, *I will raise up for Myself.* God is interested in individuals who are totally committed to Him and are willing to live for His glory. He seeks *a faithful priest*, a faithful worshiper who will protect the fire from going out. He desires someone *who will do according to what is in My heart and mind.* The essence of dwelling in His presence is doing according to what He desires.

The first person the Lord raised up was David. When He found David the king, worshiper, shepherd, warrior, and protector, He said, "I have found David son of Jesse, a man after my own heart; he will do everything I want him to do" (Acts 13:22). After David was anointed for the third time to become king over Israel, the first thing he did was bring back the presence of God to the nation of Israel. He gathered the nation and said, "Let us bring the ark of our God back to us, for we did not inquire of it during the reign of Saul" (1 Chronicles 13:3). King Saul had ruled the nation for forty years without the presence of God. David, a man after God's heart, made it his priority to bring back the Ark of God's presence as part of his commitment to serve among the people whom he was anointed to shepherd and lead.

The nation was overwhelmed with great joy when the Ark was restored to Israel, but they didn't follow the written Word of the Lord while bringing the Ark home. Instead of consecrating priests to carry the Ark, they placed it on a cart. Then, "Uzzah reached out his hand to steady the ark, because the oxen stumbled. The LORD's anger burned against Uzzah, and He struck him down because he had put his hand on the ark" (1 Chronicles 13:9–10).

I believe one of the reasons why the Lord's anger burned against Uzzah was because he took God's presence for granted. One of the things God doesn't tolerate is for us to get used to the things of the Lord. This includes losing a holy reverence for who He is by becoming lukewarm, like the church of Laodicea. When we become familiar with God's presence, we can slide away.

In the New Testament, Mary and Joseph started taking Jesus to the Temple every year. However, after twelve years it became an annual ritual for them. When Jesus was twelve years old, they inadvertently left Him in Jerusalem, assuming that He was still with them. They didn't miss His presence, and they didn't even realize they had left Him behind, until they reached their lodging place for the night.

The redemptive aspect of this story is that once Mary and Joseph discovered that Jesus wasn't with them, they didn't pretend or hide it. Instead, they stopped their journey and went back to look for Him until they found Him. It is amazingly easy to lose God's presence and pretend not to notice, but the most important thing is to repent, go back, and look for Him.

Impossible to Live without His Presence

After Uzzah's death, David was afraid to bring the Ark of the Lord to Jerusalem. However, Obed-Edom took the Ark of the Lord into his home. "The ark of God remained with the family of Obed-Edom in his house for three months, and the LORD blessed his household and everything he had" (1 Chronicles 13:14). Obed-Edom was a Gittite and understood how to dwell in the presence of God. Within three months, the supernatural blessings of the Lord overtook him because of the presence of God (see Deuteronomy 28). This became known throughout the nation, and the report reached King David.

David went to God and found out what had gone wrong. I am sure he was bewildered by the death of Uzzah and by the special supernatural blessings on the house of Obed-Edom. The Lord showed David how the problem was that they had used the wrong method to do the right thing. In correcting that past mistake, they could bring back the Ark from Obed-Edom's house to Jerusalem. For the blessings of his nation, David took the following actions:

- First, David prepared a place for the Ark. Before we try to host God's presence, we ought to prepare a worthy place for Him in our lives, homes, churches, and city. We do this by making Him the center of everything we do through our attitude and prayer.

- Second, David consecrated the priests to carry the Ark in the right way. He said, "It was because you, the Levites, did not bring it up the first time that the LORD our God broke out in anger against us. We did not inquire of Him about how to do it in the prescribed way" (1 Chronicles 15:13). He reestablished the earlier biblical standards of handling the presence of God.

- Third, David himself became one of the worshipers, like a priest, when he put on priestly garments instead of kingly robes: "Now David was clothed in a robe of fine linen, as were all the Levites who were carrying the Ark, and as were the musicians" (1 Chronicles 15:27). Furthermore, he made sacrifices as part of his worship after every six steps, and as part of self-evaluation.

- Fourth, David wrote and sang a new song to the Lord as they were bringing the Ark back (see 1 Chronicles 16).

- Fifth, David went home to bless his family. In other words, he brought a public glory to his house.

Dwelling in God's presence is the call for everyone. God is not only dwelling with us, but He is also dwelling in us by the Holy Spirit. The Word of God tells us not to grieve the Holy Spirit, and not to put out His fire. That means in the New Testament, the most important factor to abiding in the presence of God is having a pure and sensitive heart. "So, as the Holy Spirit says: 'Today, if you hear his voice, do not harden your hearts as you did in the rebellion, during the time of testing in the wilderness'" (Hebrews 3:7–8).

The Lord promised the Israelites that He would take out their stony hearts and give them hearts of flesh, so they could hear and respond to the voice of the Holy Spirit. When the Ark of the Covenant was captured, the Lord's hand was heavy on the Philistines, so they decided to send it back. Jerusalem had burned down, and there wasn't a place to put the Ark. The Mercy Seat didn't exist anymore, so they put the Ark on stone: "The Levites took down the ark of the LORD, together with the chest containing the gold objects, and placed them on the large rock" (1 Samuel 6:15). No wonder the Lord promised to take out a hard heart of stone and give us a pure, loving, and merciful heart to dwell in His presence.

If you are serious about living in God's presence, it's time to cry to the Lord, as David did, "Create in me a pure heart, O God, and renew a steadfast spirit within me" (Psalm 51:10). Become desperate for His presence, like Moses: "If your Presence does not go with us, do not send us up from here" (Exodus 33:15). Decide, like Paul, "I want to know Christ—yes, to know the power of his resurrection and participation in his sufferings, becoming like him in his death" (Philippians 3:10).

Once a person starts abiding in God's presence, it's impossible to live without it. Obed-Edom couldn't live without the presence of God after hosting it in his home for only three months. He decided to follow the Ark, and he became the gatekeeper of the tent (see 1 Chronicles 15:18, 24; 16:38).

How desperate are you for the presence of God? Are you willing to let go of your comfort and become the gatekeeper in the tent of His presence? He longs for relationship with you:

God first intervened to choose a people for his name from the Gentiles. The words of the prophets are in agreement with this, as it is written:

> After this I will return and rebuild David's fallen tent. Its ruins I will rebuild, and I will restore it, that the rest of mankind may seek the Lord, even all the Gentiles who bear my name, says the Lord, who does these things—things known from long ago.
>
> Acts 15:14–18

Questions for Abiding Deeper

- Have you gone through a period of purification, as the Israelites did at the foot of Mount Sinai? How did you do that, and what was it like for you?
- When do you feel a strong desire for the presence of God, or have you not yet felt that tug on your heart?

7

SEEKING GOD'S FACE

ALEMU BEEFTU

Such is the generation of those who seek him, who seek your face, God of Jacob.

Psalm 24:6

God is looking for someone who reflects the glory of His face. Every person is born with God's preplanned purpose, or prophetic destiny, within him or her. Each person's purpose is prophetic as God has called it into existence in advance, a uniquely created destiny well-orchestrated by the Creator Himself. In other words, God has a plan for you and me, just as He told the nation of Israel: "I know the plans I have for you . . . plans to prosper you and not to harm you, plans to give you hope and a future" (Jeremiah 29:11).

Every generation and every nation has a prophetic destiny that God expects to be fulfilled. True personal fulfillment and lasting joy come from discovering God's promises and accomplishing them with wholehearted devotion to Him. This prophetic destiny is both a plan and a promise from God for those who obey His will. God declares the name and purpose He has for each one of us before our birth and reveals it in the process, according to His timetable. Isaiah 49:1 states that He mentions our name in our mother's womb. He establishes our identity before our birth. Knowing and accepting that identity is the foundation for fulfilling your personal prophetic destiny.

In prophetic worship, David described a generation with prophetic destiny: "*This is the generation* [description] of those *who seek Him* [who inquire of and for Him and of necessity require Him], *who seek Your face, [O God of] Jacob*" (Psalm 24:6 AMPC, emphasis added).

This is not about being purpose driven, as much as it is about needing to do His will daily. A person isn't driven by purpose, but is driven by the Person and life of Jesus Christ. God didn't promise to be found when we seek what we can accomplish for Him. His promise is that if we seek Him wholeheartedly, we will find Him. David identified these character traits that make a generation different from the rest: *the pursuit of God*, and *spiritual hunger*, including *a hunger for God's Word*. Let's look at these traits more closely.

The Pursuit of God

When the psalmist writes, "This is the generation of those who seek Him," the Hebrew word for seeking here is *darash* (*daw-rash'*). Various lexicons translate this as pursuing in search of, asking or inquiring after, desiring, requiring, making inquisition, endeavoring, and questioning.[1] At the beginning of His earthly ministry, Jesus told His audience to *seek* (desire, endeavor, inquire after, require) the Kingdom of God. A generation with character is marked by seeking God more than anything else. Seeking comes from true hunger for the presence and righteousness of God. "My heart says of you, 'Seek His face!' Your face, LORD, I will seek" (Psalm 27:8).

When we seek the Lord out of true spiritual thirst and longing for Him, He satisfies us with His manifested presence. David said, "As for me, I will continue beholding Your face in righteousness (rightness, justice, and right standing with You); I shall be fully satisfied, when I awake [to find myself] beholding Your form [and having sweet communion with You]" (Psalm 17:15 AMPC).

The prayer of those who pursue God is not to receive what they want, but to see His face and stand in His presence. At this point, it is very crucial to understand the difference between *asking, seeking,* and *knocking. Asking* is for the purpose of meeting our daily needs, which is important. But it is usually limited to temporary things. "For the things we see now will soon be gone, but the things we cannot see will last forever" (2 Corinthians 4:18 NLT).

Then there is *seeking,* which helps those who are pursuing God to order their priorities. That was the reason why Jesus told the disciples, "But seek first his kingdom and his righteousness, and all these things will be given to you as well" (Matthew 6:33). Those who seek the Lord honor Him with their lives by making His will the priority in their prayers. These types of prayers are deeper and more profound, not concentrating on our daily needs since the Lord knows those before we do.

Finally, there is *knocking.* God opens the door for a person who knocks, and He extends a warm welcome, an invitation to come in for friendship, fellowship, and communion. The Lord's desire is for us to go and knock at the throne room, and enter His presence to see the King of Glory in His beauty. "Your eyes will see the king in his beauty and view a land that stretches afar" (Isaiah 33:17).

We enter His gates with thanksgiving and adoration to worship Him, see Him in His majesty, and receive His mercy and grace. Under an open heaven, we need to go higher to see what we haven't seen and hear what we haven't heard: "After this I looked, and there before me was a door standing open in heaven. And the voice I had first heard speaking to me like a trumpet said, 'Come up here, and I will show you what must take place after this'" (Revelation 4:1).

Spiritual Hunger

Spiritual hunger is the foundation for pursuing God. The most dangerous obstacle in a Christian's walk is losing his or her appetite for the things of God.

The Lord invites His people to come and eat freely. Both hunger and malnutrition are enemies of spiritual maturity. This is the reason God invites His people to come and eat with Him throughout the Bible: "Come, all you who are thirsty, come to the waters; and you who have no money, come, buy and eat! Come, buy wine and milk without money and without cost" (Isaiah 55:1).

Hunger is described this way in *The International Standard Bible Encyclopedia*:

> **HUNGER,** huṇ'gēr (רָעֵב, rā'ābh; λιμός, limós (subs.), πεινάω, peináō (vb.): (1) The desire for food, a physiological sensation associated with emptiness of the stomach, and dependent on some state of the mucous membrane; (2) starvation as the effect of want of food, as Exodus 16:3; Isaiah 49:10; (3) to feel the craving for food as Deuteronomy 8:3; when used to indicate the condition due to general scarcity of food as Jeremiah 38:9; Ezekiel 34:29. It is replaced in KJV RV by "famine." The word is used to express the poverty which follows idleness and laziness (Proverbs 19:15). The absence of this condition is given as one of the characteristics of the future state of happiness (Isaiah 49:10; Ezekiel 34:29; Revelation 7:16). Metaphorically the passionate striving for moral and spiritual rectitude is called hungering and thirsting after righteousness (Matthew 5:6); and the satisfaction of the soul which receives Christ is described as a state in which "he shall not hunger" (John 6:35).[2]

The currency of the Kingdom is a true hunger for the things of the Lord. While a lack of appetite for the things of the Lord leads to hunger, a lack of discernment results in malnutrition (not having the knowledge or determination to choose healthy, spiritual nourishment).

For the Food and Agriculture Organization of the United Nations (FAO), the definition of hunger is when "caloric intake is below the minimum dietary energy requirement (MDER). The MDER is the amount of energy needed to perform light activity and to maintain a minimum acceptable weight for attained height."[3] Hunger is different from malnutrition, which the FAO describes as "deficiencies, excesses or imbalances in the consumption of macro- and/or micro-nutrients."[4]

Personally, I have experienced both physical and spiritual hunger. Physical hunger is easier to tolerate when a person's spiritual appetite is satisfied. As a boy who grew up in the countryside of Ethiopia, physical and spiritual hunger were not new to me. What was new was that I didn't know I was spiritually hungry until I heard the Gospel for the first time. One time when I was in the second grade, a math teacher read Psalm 15 to open the class. The first verse asks a question: "LORD, who may dwell in your sacred tent? Who may live on your holy mountain?"

It was clear to me that I couldn't dwell in God's presence, and the Lord opened my eyes and showed me what hell is. I began to shake, and I shook for the entire class. I knew I had to do something in response to the God of this psalm. After class, I went to the teacher and asked, "Sir, what is the answer to what you read?"

He told me, "Don't worry about it, because it isn't part of the curriculum. I just felt led to read it."

Searching for a missionary who could help me, I turned to the school's interim director and asked her about Psalm 15. I didn't tell her about my classroom experience, but she understood what was happening inside me. She shared the Gospel with me right then, sitting under the flagpole. After she explained the Gospel and the way of salvation, she asked me if I wanted to accept the Lord as my personal Savior.

I said, "Yes, I would!"

She said, "Let's go to one of the classrooms, and I will pray with you."

To her surprise, I said no—meaning I didn't want to take the time to go to a classroom. I didn't want to wait another minute to know that I was saved! I said, "If everything you said is true, I don't want to wait to know I am saved."

Right then and there, she read Romans 10:9 to me: "If you declare with your mouth, 'Jesus is Lord,' and believe in your heart that God raised him from the dead, you will be saved." Then she led me in prayer, and I accepted the Lord at fourteen years old. (My country's grades were different from America's school system, so I was fourteen in "second grade.")

That day marked a turning point in my life—my true break from the past and into the future with God. My spirit was settled in me that day. My spiritual hunger was satisfied in the Lord. Although I didn't understand the full implications of my decision, it placed me on a path to desire more of God and His truth. I was the first person in my family to go to school, and the first to accept Jesus Christ as Lord and Savior. Until we have a true relationship with God through the forgiveness of sin, we won't fully understand spiritual satisfaction.

After my greatest spiritual satisfaction, I faced a serious challenge that resulted in physical hunger. Because of my faith in Jesus, my aunt's husband told me, "You can't stay with us since you refuse to worship my idol in the house."

My father had been providing supplies to feed me while I lived with my aunt, but the supplies didn't come as my aunt anticipated, so I didn't have regular meals. I went to school without breakfast every day, and during lunch hour when students went home for lunch, I went to a nearby river. Most of the time I bowed by the water to kneel and pray, as if that were my well-prepared meal. I drank the water before the afternoon class. Most of the week, that was my breakfast, lunch, and dinner for two to three days. As I look back, Jesus did for me what He did at the wedding at Cana in Galilee by changing water into wine. The miracle He did for me is even greater because He changed dirty water into the best food.

After I took a water baptism class, I was baptized in that same river. I was so spiritually satisfied that I didn't look at my physical hunger as a price for remaining in relationship with the Lord. His presence was real, and His miracle was undeniable. I was hungrier for His spiritual food and more desperate for the Word of God.

Spiritual hunger causes us to focus on God. Establishing Him as a priority means letting go of other things and living for His revealed will. True spiritual hunger starts with a strong desire to know the Lord, His ways, and His perfect will through the written Word. The knowledge of God's Word is the foundation for knowing His perfect will. Paul states,

> But whatever was to my profit I now consider loss for the sake of Christ. What is more, I consider everything a loss compared to the surpassing greatness of knowing Christ Jesus my Lord, for whose sake I have lost all things. I consider them rubbish, that I may gain Christ.
>
> Philippians 3:7–8 NIV1984

When we make God the highest priority in our lives, we remove every hindrance that stops us from running to Him and for Him. In every generation, those who made His presence their dwelling place separated themselves from others by letting go of the things that tried to entangle them. They focused on what was most important to the call of being conformed into the image of Christ. The Word of God says,

> Since we are surrounded by so great a cloud of witnesses [who have born testimony to the Truth], let us strip off and throw aside every

encumbrance (unnecessary weight) and that sin which so readily (deftly and cleverly) clings to and entangles us, and let us run with patient endurance and steady and active persistence the appointed course of the race that is set before us.

Hebrews 12:1 AMPC

When I first came to the Lord, committing to pay the price to follow Him was called "the cost of discipleship." I don't hear that phrase often in this generation. When a person is hungry for God and His Word, whatever the cost might be, it becomes insignificant in light of knowing Him and being in His presence. I witnessed this in my own life as a young believer. What follows is the story of how I started this journey of seeking God and His Word more than my safety.

A serious conflict occurred between my father and me after I accepted the Lord in second grade at missionary school. After I accepted the Lord as my personal Savior, I went home for Christmas break and my entire family had gathered there. As usual, my family's traditional celebration included Christmas traditions mixed with idol worship. A sheep was slaughtered and prepared, and each of us stood in line to receive a portion. I knew the sheep had been offered to and "blessed by" an idol that my parents worshiped out of fear. I didn't have much knowledge about idol worship, but I felt strongly in my heart that I should not eat the meat my father was serving us.

Since I am the youngest, I was the last in line to be served. I respected my father, but when it was my turn to receive a portion of the meat, I couldn't take it. I was suddenly face-to-face with the conflict expressed in 2 Corinthians 6:16–17: "What agreement is there between the temple of God and idols? For we are the temple of the living God. . . . 'Come out from among them and be separate, says the Lord. Touch no unclean thing, and I will receive you.'"

When my father saw that I wasn't coming to take the meat, he wondered what was going on. He said, "Come and take it."

I responded in an unwise tone of voice, "Now I am a Christian, and I don't want to eat what is offered to an idol."

My father believed that he was also a Christian, because the Coptic religion in our region is Christianity mixed with indigenous beliefs. He was deeply offended by my words, and this usually gentle man became livid with rage and picked up his spear. My own father, whom I dearly loved, was about to kill me!

Thankfully, one of my brothers intervened, saying, "He's only a boy! You can discipline him and get him to change his mind. You don't have to kill him!"

During the rest of the vacation, I avoided my father as he stewed in anger. He decided that I shouldn't go back to the missionary school. I was a newborn believer, beginning to read the Bible, and I knew I had to pray. Since I didn't have a place for prayer, I hid in a forest of banana trees that had no fruit. That became my "Upper Room" for many years, whenever I was at home.

During the rainy season, it was difficult to kneel in the mud for prayer, but I didn't know if God could hear me if I prayed standing up. I would kneel in that wet, muddy place, but I had the greatest joy of my life, because I knew prayer worked. All I wanted was to talk to God and feel His presence.

I prayed during the remainder of that Christmas break when my father and I first disagreed. I wasn't ready to give up my education. I was determined to return to school, even if it meant going without my father's approval and support. Somehow, I knew this was about my future. This was the relationship I couldn't live without! At the end of the vacation, I went back to school without telling my parents.

When I returned to school, my aunt, who had been giving me room and board, found out about the conflict between my father and me. She waited a few days for supplies to be sent from my parents. In the meantime, my aunt's husband organized a special celebration and worship night for his idols. He asked me to help with the preparation for idol worship. I told him that since I was a believer in Jesus Christ, I didn't want to help him worship false gods. He told my aunt, "He cannot stay here any longer."

My aunt told me, "You no longer can live under my roof."

That was the most challenging night of my life. The next morning, I went to school as usual, not knowing what would happen when the school day was over. At school, I pretended everything was okay. However, it wasn't long before the school director, Miss Cane, noticed that something was bothering me. Finally, she got the story out of me that I had no place to live. She told me about a nearby dorm for boys who lived far from the school. She arranged for me to work for her every day after school and on weekends to pay for my room, food, and other expenses.

A Hunger for God's Word

School, housing, and food were covered the day I started working for Miss Cane. But as a new believer, I was hungry for the Word of God more than anything. I had a strong desire to buy my own Bible. I told Miss Cane I planned to save money to buy a Bible, and she told me I could earn that too. But a schoolboy who must work for his schooling and living expenses doesn't end up with much extra money. One year later, I still didn't have a Bible. Miss Cane counted my money and told me I had only half of the needed amount.

I envisioned another year without having the Word of God. I was so sad and disappointed, tears started running down my cheeks. Seeing the depth of my disappointment, the director gave me a Bible that evening. What a joyful night! That night, I didn't sleep. I read my new Bible all night long. My roommate was unhappy because I stayed up all night, but I didn't pay any attention to him. My hunger for the Word was being filled! I loved the Word of God, and I love it now.

A teachable spirit is one of the key elements in breaking out from the old and entering into the new. As a new believer, I had a huge desire to know and learn the Word of God. Miss Bea Colman, a missionary wife and Sunday school teacher, started teaching a weekly discipleship class that she called Sunday School. There were five of us, but she prepared lessons as if she taught a large, important class. During the summer, I went home and helped my father on the family farm, which meant I wasn't at school. So on Sundays I would get up very early and walk many miles to attend this Sunday School and church. Since it was the rainy season, I always arrived soaking wet. I went to the toilet room to wring the water out of my clothes and put them back on. Later, when I arrived back home, I went straight to the herds and came home with the cows after dark. My parents didn't know where I had been. I was always very hungry by nightfall because I hadn't eaten all day! But I had a powerful joy because of my spiritual satisfaction.

The night I received my Bible at school and started to read it, I loved it so much that I didn't want to stop. However, before that, the first time a teacher had asked me to share for school devotions I didn't have a Bible yet, so I had to borrow one. I didn't know the difference between the Old and New Testaments, or the order of the books. When I shared that first devotion, I didn't close the book until I finished, because I wouldn't have been able to find the passage I was talking about again. That day, I decided to know the Scripture when I had my own Bible, and I promised the Lord that I would keep my passion for the Word of God as long as I live.

Yes! "Such is the generation of those who seek him, who seek your face, God of Jacob" (Psalm 24:6). When God sees a generation that seeks Him more than any other thing and is willing to pay the price for following the King of glory, He declares, "This is the generation!" Throughout all of history, God has been looking for a generation that seeks Him. He looks for those with hungry hearts. One of the signs the Lord looks for in every generation is *a heart that seeks Him.*

QUESTIONS FOR ABIDING DEEPER

- Do you recall a time in your life when you deeply hungered after God's presence and His Word? What resulted from that time of seeking?
- Are you seeking God now? Are you willing to pay the price to further His Kingdom in your generation?

8

SEEKING GOD'S PRESENCE

ALEMU BEEFTU

Seek the Lord and the strength he gives. Seek his presence continually!

Psalm 105:4 NET

God is looking for someone willing to reveal the glory of His manifested presence. Seeking God's face is all about entering a transformational relationship with Him. If we don't actively seek Him, we won't find Him. As we have observed in Enoch's life, God enjoys our fellowship with Him more than anything we have worked hard for. He created human beings for this level of fellowship.

When God called to Adam and Eve, it was the expression of His desire for us to be in His presence: "Then the man and his wife heard the sound of the LORD God as he was walking in the garden in the cool of the day" (Genesis 3:8). That desire has never stopped. It's no wonder that God took Enoch to walk with Him, Abraham to be His friend, and David to be a man after His own heart. Enoch and

Abraham walked with God as friends, but David made a commitment to seek God's presence all his life: "When my heart whispered, 'Seek God,' my whole being replied, 'I'm seeking him!'" (Psalm 27:8 MSG). Jacob had been on a journey to find his prophetic destiny since birth. He had pressed onward for many years before he reached Peniel, where he saw God face-to-face (see Genesis 32:22–32). Finally, at Peniel he received a new name as a sign of blessing from God, and breakthrough to reach his destination.

Peniel means "the face of God." The face of God is His presence, majesty, glory, and power. Seeking the face of God is the goal for a generation with a prophetic destiny. Jacob arrived at his prophetic destiny after he had this powerful, special encounter with God. Moses spent forty days and nights on a mountain in God's presence, and when he came down from the mountain, his face was shining with God's glory (see Exodus 34:28–29).

When we seek God's hand, we seek provision and relate to Him as our provider, guide, deliverer, protector, etc. Jesus' role in our lives is to be the Good Shepherd. We enter this covenant relationship by knowing Him and accepting Him as our Savior and High Priest. That's the foundation of our salvation. We can say with all sincerity, "The LORD is my shepherd; there is nothing I lack. He lets me lie down in green pastures; He leads me beside quiet waters. He renews my life; He leads me along the right paths for His name's sake" (Psalm 23:1–3 HCSB).

In Psalm 23, God is our Good Shepherd, and we are in a covenant relationship with Him. However, in Psalm 24, He is the Creator, Lord of the universe, and King of glory. A generation with a prophetic destiny understands and stands on its covenant foundation.

A Step of Faith

Once the covenant is established, crossing over to be in the presence of the King becomes the first part of our spiritual war. Just like the Egyptians, Amalekites, Moabites, and other physical forces who tried to stop the Israelites from going into the Promised Land, Satan tries to stop us spiritually from reaching our prophetic destiny. Spiritual war is just part of moving forward to reach our destination. In our case, Satan tries to make us afraid to cross over to be in the presence of the King, so that we miss out on receiving authority.

Yes, a journey of crossing over is very frightening because of the valley we must go through. "Yes, though I walk through the [deep, sunless] valley of the shadow of death, I will fear or dread no evil, for You are with me; Your rod [to protect] and Your staff [to guide], they comfort me" (Psalm 23:4 AMPC). The valley is what lies between the pasture and the table of the King.

Yet our God is a God of victory. When we engage in spiritual war, it's by faith, for victory, for our destiny, and it's for the glory of the King. Victory gives us authority to open the gates for the King of glory, who is the Lord of hosts, strong and mighty in battle. In a battle of destiny, we are more than conquerors: "Yet amid all these things we are more than conquerors and gain a surpassing victory through Him Who loved us" (Romans 8:37 AMPC).

When we are in the field or pasture, everything is about our needs, just like the sheep in the field in Psalm 23. However, once we step forward and sit at the table with the King of glory, our purpose is fellowshiping with Him. We must open our heart to Him before we can open the ancient gates for Him. His voice is calling for us to open the door for Him to come into fellowship with us. Once we enter that kind of fellowship, our desire changes, and we focus on fulfilling the desires of the King.

Kings express their desires in close fellowship with their trusted servants, who sit at their tables with them. Those who are trusted as friends sit at a king's table and pay close attention to the expressed desire of their king. They listen carefully. After the formal dinner is over, the trusted servants go out to implement what the king has expressed as his heart's desire.

When we seek God's face, we relate to Him as our King and Lord to honor and worship Him. We declare not only what He does for us, but who He is and what He deserves as our Creator, Redeemer, Lord, and King: "To him who sits on the throne and to the Lamb be praise and honor and glory and power, for ever and ever! The four living creatures said, 'Amen,' and the elders fell down and worshiped" (Revelation 5:13–14).

Seeking God requires a true desire to exalt Him through worship. This desire creates a burning passion to be in His presence. David put it this way: "You have said, Seek My face [inquire for and require My presence as your vital need]. My heart says to You, Your face (Your presence), Lord, will I seek, inquire for, and require [of necessity and on the authority of Your Word]" (Psalm 27:8 AMPC).

Worship Produces an Aroma

The worship that flows from this desire and longing is aromatic to God. That's the kind of worship the wise men brought to the Lord Jesus (see Matthew 2). Led by passion to come and worship Jesus, they were anticipating His birth. When the time came, they were prepared to go on a long journey and worship Him. They prepared gifts to honor the King. They were willing to pay the price by taking that arduous journey. Their focus was to go and worship. A journey of many days, weeks, or even years didn't discourage them, and they traveled at night so they could see His star.

Arriving in Jerusalem, the wise men asked, "Where is He Who has been born King of the Jews?" (Matthew 2:2 AMPC). They had clear focus and only one purpose: to worship the King. When they found Him in Bethlehem, they were overjoyed. The Bible says, "Let all those that seek and require You rejoice and be glad in You; let such as love Your salvation say continually, The Lord be magnified!" (Psalm 40:16 AMPC).

After they worshiped Jesus, the wise men opened their treasure boxes and gave Him gifts. True worship means that we open every box in our life. By opening their treasure boxes, the wise men declared Him as the owner of everything. He was worthy of their best gifts. They had nothing to hide, and neither do we. We are dependent on Him for our very existence. That's true worship. Every box we open in God's presence will be used for His glory. God desires the generation that wants to come and worship Him and be in His presence, opening every box that has been locked. That includes spiritual gifts, material possessions, emotional hurts, and wounds. When we are in His presence, we can safely be vulnerable, because we are covered by His mercy and grace.

Seeking God's face is all about being in His presence. That's where His glory shines on us. That's why He commanded the high priest to cover His people with this blessing: "The LORD bless you and keep you; the LORD make *his face shine* on you and be gracious to you; the LORD *turn his face* toward you and give you peace" (Numbers 6:24–26, emphasis added).

In God's presence, when His face shines on us, His glory covers us. Since He dwells in an unapproachable, glorious light of holiness, beauty, power, strength, and majesty, we receive impartation that transforms us from glory to glory, into His likeness. It also encourages us to seek His presence more: "Seek the Lord and the strength he gives. Seek his presence continually!" (Psalm 105:4 NET).

The God of Jacob is the God of prophetic destiny. I believe no one has fought for his or her prophetic destiny the way Jacob did. Jacob was mostly misunderstood by his own family, and later by others, yet he received his prophetic destiny before he was born. His father, Isaac, prayed for a child, and his mother, Rebekah, became pregnant. It was an unusual pregnancy, as two boys started wrestling for their prophetic destiny within Rebekah's womb. When she asked the Lord what was going on, He told her, "Two nations are in your womb; two people will come from you and be separated.

One people will be stronger than the other, and the older will serve the younger" (Genesis 25:23 HCSB).

In other words, the younger, who turned out to be Jacob, would become a leader. That prophecy entered Jacob's spirit in his mother's womb, and from that time on, he started fighting for that prophetic destiny. He was born with a prophetic destiny, although he didn't understand it, as is the case for every person. That prophetic destiny became the driving force in Jacob's life, making him a wrestler or fighter, as well as a restless man.

Prophetic Destiny Brought to Light

A person can't have true rest until the realization of what God has created him or her to accomplish is brought to light. God reveals prophetic destiny to individuals in different ways and at different stages of life, but everyone is born with a purpose. That's one of the reasons why Psalm 24:6 talks about "seeking the God of Jacob" instead of the God of Abraham or Isaac. We know that the name "God of Abraham" refers to the God of covenant. Abraham is the one who received the covenant and walked with God. God is also called the "God of Isaac," which can mean the God of promises or blessings. Abraham received the covenant, and Isaac received the blessings of the covenant. Jacob, on the other hand, received his prophetic destiny and later entered the full revelation of his destiny for future blessings. The things God promised both Abraham and Isaac were fully realized in Jacob. The covenant nation was called by Jacob's prophetic destiny name, Israel, as a picture of new identity.

Seeking the God of Jacob means seeking our prophetic destiny without giving up due to challenges along the way. The starting point in fulfilling our prophetic destiny is to hear clearly what God has said. The call of God is unchangeable. God doesn't change His mind about our destiny, since He created us for that very purpose.

In fact, He called us by our prophetic names and honored us as individuals before we were born (see Isaiah 49:1–5).

The prophetic word—or your call of God—is your weapon to fight against everything that tries to stop you from reaching your destiny. We usually refer to this as "hearing the call of God." Once we receive a revelation of God's plan for our lives and embrace that plan, we are on our way. In some cases, the Lord places that prophetic destiny in a person and it becomes like a burning fire within. God gives some individuals a burden for things related to their prophetic destiny, and that makes them restless. God uses that restlessness to guide them to their prophetic destiny, just like Jacob.

For Moses, the burden was for God's people. He was willing to give up everything—title, pleasure, opportunities, and fame—because of the fire of prophetic destiny in him. Although Moses didn't have a direct encounter with God until he was eighty years old, he was driven by prophetic destiny. On the other hand, Jeremiah heard his prophetic destiny when he was young and was encouraged by the Lord to embrace his purpose. David also learned about his prophetic destiny and was anointed when he was young.

The Lord has revealed prophetic destinies in different ways throughout history. William Wilberforce, a British statesman and reformer, knew that his God-given destiny was to abolish the brutal British slave trade. In the late 1700s and early 1800s, Wilberforce fought and won a heroic, twenty-year battle against slavery that changed history. President Abraham Lincoln was inspired when he read about Wilberforce's perseverance, and he later led the United States through the Civil War, which preserved the Union and abolished slavery in America. Lincoln's destiny was fulfilled, costing him his own life near the end of the war. Lincoln was a humble man of God who was often maligned and misunderstood for his moral standards and determination to free a race of people and a nation.

Paying the Price

Bestselling author Eric Metaxas released a book titled *Bonhoeffer: Pastor, Martyr, Prophet, Spy* (Thomas Nelson, 2010) that is a brilliant biography of Dietrich Bonhoeffer. The book reveals a man who truly sought God's face and demonstrated supernatural courage and faith in the face of the monstrous evil perpetrated by Adolf Hitler and his Nazi regime. Bonhoeffer was safe in the United States but chose to return to Germany and stand with the persecuted Church. He did everything in his power to smuggle Jews into neutral Switzerland and even participated in plans to overthrow the Nazi regime. One endorser of Metaxas's book described Bonhoeffer as "a clear-headed, deeply convicted Christian who submitted to no one and nothing except God and his Word."[1]

Bonhoeffer was imprisoned, and then he was executed by direct order of Hitler on April 7, 1945, just two weeks before the Allied forces liberated his fellow prisoners. Through it all, Bonhoeffer sought God. A German doctor who witnessed Bonhoeffer's death later wrote,

> Through the half-open door in one room of the huts, I saw Pastor Bonhoeffer . . . kneeling on the floor praying fervently to his God. I was most deeply moved by the way this lovable man prayed, so devout and so certain that God heard his prayer. . . . In the almost fifty years that I worked as a doctor, I have hardly ever seen a man die so entirely submissive to the will of God.[2]

We each have a prophetic destiny that God has ordained for us. We must seek Him fervently and allow Him to lead us into our calling and purpose in His timing. We are not all called to dramatic destinies like Wilberforce or Bonhoeffer, but God's purpose for each of us is equally important in His eyes.

Removing Hinderances

A willingness to let go of the past and seek God wholeheartedly is one character trait of a generation with passion and fire for God. There are some things we need to let go of as we seek Him. For example, we need to discard our old nature, take off our old shoes, remove our old garments, and set aside wrong armor. Let's look a little more closely at these, which are the kinds of things this generation should consider removing or taking off—both to run to God and also to run the race set before us.

Discarding the Old Nature

When a person accepts Christ, that person becomes a new creation. In other words, the old sin nature has been removed and is replaced by a new nature. A person completes this process by submitting to the Holy Spirit and resisting the works of the flesh. Paul summarized this process:

> Strip yourselves of your former nature [put off and discard your old unrenewed self] which characterized your previous manner of life and becomes corrupt through lusts and desires that spring from delusion; and be constantly renewed in the spirit of your mind [having a fresh mental and spiritual attitude].
>
> Ephesians 4:22–23 AMPC

In this context, taking off the old nature means letting go of the sin we practiced in the past, and renewing our mind by the Word and Spirit of God.

In his book *Rebel with a Cause*, Franklin Graham shares his testimony of how he had to make a choice to cast off his old sin nature to fulfill his prophetic destiny and carry forward his generation's evangelistic call. Growing up in the shadow of his father, Dr. Billy Graham, Franklin was a fun-loving, free-spirited young man who admits that he had a knowledge of God while skating on a slippery pathway of sin. In the book, he tells about a time in July 1974 when he was working on his father's logistics team for an evangelistic conference in Switzerland:

> Even though I was living one adventure after another, I felt such emptiness. I had friends, but still I was lonely and unfulfilled. Something just didn't connect in my life. It was like having a television but not plugging it in. The sinful life I was living was not satisfying me any longer. . . . The truth was I felt miserable because my life wasn't right with God.
>
> During the conference, I celebrated my twenty-second birthday. Mama and Daddy wanted to take me to lunch. . . . After the meal, Daddy and I walked along a pathway beside the lake. My father, who hates confrontation, said: "Franklin, your mother and I sense there's a struggle going on in your life."
>
> He had caught me totally off guard. *How does he know this?* I wondered.
>
> Daddy continued saying, "You're going to have to make a choice either to accept Christ or reject Him. You can't continue to play the middle ground. Either you're going to choose to follow and obey Him or reject Him."
>
> After he had his say, Daddy patted my shoulder and smiled. He said nothing more about it as we finished our walk.[3]

Franklin admitted that initially, he was angry. He thought he had been clever and had fooled his parents. He had attended church and said the right words, but obviously his sinful life was uncovered. Over the next few weeks he pondered his father's words, sought wise counsel, and pored over the Scriptures. He had made a decision for Christ as a child, but he finally had to admit that he had been running from God for years. After searching his soul and acknowledging that sin had gained control in his life, he knelt beside his bed and asked God to forgive and cleanse him. Then he invited the Lord, by faith, to come into his life. The rebel stopped running that very night. Franklin Graham cast off that old sin nature, and today his ministry, Samaritan's Purse, continues to impact millions of lives around the world.

Taking Off Old Shoes

Old shoes symbolize old experiences or a walk of life that cannot carry us to our prophetic destiny. After Moses accepted his prophetic destiny and waited for eighty years, the first thing God asked him to do at the burning bush was to take off his shoes (see Exodus 3:5). Moses' shoes were a picture of how a long period of waiting can create hope-deferred disappointment, rejection, fear, frustration, etc. After Moses took off his shoes, the Lord sent him back to Egypt to set God's people free from 430 years of slavery. He went back not as a criminal, but as a deliverer, stepping into his prophetic destiny.

God also told Joshua to take off his shoes before taking victory over Jericho (see Joshua 5:15). In Joshua's case, his shoes were a reminder of forty years of wandering in the desert. Moses took off his shoes to bring God's people out of Egypt, while Joshua took off his shoes to walk Israel into their inheritance by defeating their enemies. Joshua took off his shoes as a sign of submission to the Lord, and ultimately he took the people into the Promised Land by defeating those who occupied it. That was Joshua's prophetic destiny; he was born for that purpose.

My own prophetic destiny required me to run away from my family farm in the Ethiopian countryside at the age of twelve to attend a school that was run by Christian missionaries and was four hours from home. I had a burning desire to learn to read, but as the youngest of ten children, I was expected to work the land and nothing more. When I accepted Jesus as my Savior at fourteen, I paid the high price of being rejected by my family, but God wanted me to take off the shoes of my family's past and walk in His shoes.

Only He could provide for my education up to the doctoral level, and only He could open doors for a ministry based in the United States that would serve Christian leaders in over fifty developing countries.

Removing an Old Garment

A garment is a covering symbolizing identity. The Word of God tells us to put on Christ as our new identity. To enter our prophetic destiny, it is critical to remove our old identity for the new.

The widow Ruth left Moab to be with Naomi. After Ruth gleaned in Boaz's fields for a season, the time came for her to enter her prophetic destiny. Naomi told her to take off the old garment of Moab and put on a new garment as a sign of her new identity, so she could go to meet Boaz on the threshing floor (see Ruth 3:1–5).

In Zechariah 3, Joshua stood before the Angel of the Lord, with Satan opposing him. Joshua was dressed in filthy garments, but the Lord took them off and clothed him in rich robes. This was necessary to stop the accusation of the enemy, allowing the Lord's temple to be completed for His greater glory (see Zechariah 6:9–15). After Joshua put on the new garment, the Lord also commanded that he be crowned with an elaborate crown made of silver and gold (see verse 11). A crown is a picture of authority; crowns are for kings. Zechariah's vision prophesied the coming of the "man whose name is the Branch" (see verse 12)! When we accept our new identity, we can exercise our spiritual authority as well. However, without a new identity there is no spiritual authority or crown.

After Jesus raised Lazarus, He told others to untie him, remove the burial garments, and let him go (see John 11:44). Lazarus's garments were a symbol of unbelief and popular cultural values. The word of Jesus to Lazarus's sisters was that their brother's sickness was not for death, but for the glory of God. When Jesus didn't show up when they expected Him, however, they went ahead and buried their brother according to the cultural tradition of the time. When Jesus did arrive, He told them the first thing to do was to remove the stone of unbelief, and then remove the garment of the grave, which represented a completely wrong identity for Lazarus.

Setting Aside Wrong Armor

When David was ready to fight Goliath, King Saul put his own armor on him, but David told Saul he wouldn't be able to fight with the king's armor. Saul's armor was a picture of another person's identity and of using old methods for a new war. David took off Saul's armor before he went to fight the giant.

A generation with prophetic destiny cannot afford to put on the wrong identity to win the battle against the giants of their time and generation. Past methods may not provide the solutions for today's challenges. Any generation with prophetic destiny must take off the things that hinder.

Priorities reflect one's value system, but they must be in the right order. We seek what we value above everything else. God is looking for a generation that values His righteousness and Kingdom. He imparts His righteousness to us so we will have a right-standing position with Him. When we seek God, we seek His rule and establish a right relationship with the King, submitting to His authority as His children. We reflect the character of His Kingdom: peace, righteousness, light, truth, abundant life, the power of the Holy Spirit, and His glorious presence. We reflect God's manifested glory and are constantly transformed into a likeness of His image. When His Kingdom is within us, our desire is for Him to rule and guide our lives. This is the foundation of our prophetic call to glorify and live for God's eternal purposes.

Our prophetic call is to establish our relationship with the King of glory, to know who we are in Him, and to know our specific role in His Kingdom. This enables us to take hold of the promises of God for our lives. That will lead us into the fuller revelation of who our God is, which brings transformation to our lives. The process of this revelation will reveal our true identity as well. We will know who we are in Him, enabling us to walk in authority as the children of God in His Kingdom.

QUESTIONS FOR ABIDING DEEPER

- What are the old things that need to be removed from your life so you can step into your new calling?
- Do you know what the destiny call of God over your life is? If not, get into His presence and begin to seek that out.

9

BECOMING HIS VIP

ALEMU BEEFTU

Fear not, for I have redeemed you; I have summoned you by name;
you are mine.

Isaiah 43:2 NIV1984

*Why am I here? Does everyone have a purpose? Am I even on the right
path?*

These are some of the questions about *Value*, *Identity*, and ***Purpose*** that those in the "VIP generation" (which includes all of us alive today) ask as they seek to discover and walk out their destiny. In that seeking, we discover that there is a God-defined destiny for each of us, and that there are measurable, quantifiable outcomes that create powerful leaders. We can become such leaders, who know how to make a lasting impact, whether it's in the marketplace or the Church.

When Jesus ascended into heaven, He promised us the Holy Spirit and left us spiritual gifts. The gifts of the Holy Spirit enable us to attain the fullness of God's glory. As His people, we reflect His glory daily through our lifestyle, actions, attitudes, motives, desires, and plans. He also gave gifts to His Church so the Body of Christ can reach the fullness of His glory through the process of transformation. This process matures us, allowing us to become ambassadors for His Kingdom.

God gave five ministry callings to His Church: apostles, prophets, evangelists, pastors, and teachers. These people are gifted with leadership anointing and the authority to raise up, equip, and prepare the Body of Christ to become a mighty army for Kingdom advancement. The purpose of the fivefold leadership ministry is to restore divine order in God's Kingdom. At the beginning of creation, divine order began. God is the God of order; His nature and attributes require order to reflect His majesty as the Creator of the universe and King of glory.

No matter what humanity builds, it falls short of God's glory. Our best efforts can never compare. The only things that can reflect His glory are what has originated from the Spirit of God. What the Spirit reveals to us is a framework to follow that divine order. Without following God's pattern, the fivefold leaders can't equip a generation to reveal and reflect His glory, host His presence, and glorify Him.

The fivefold ministry must understand the Lord's divine pattern and how to raise the VIP generation. The VIP generation establishes *Value*, *Identity*, and *Purpose* for the Kingdom of God.

Establishing a Divine Pattern

The definition of a *pattern* includes a regular design, plan, or model. A pattern is a prototype that illustrates a standard manner of performance, like gunshots on a target. The blueprint a pattern provides sets a standard for future operations and helps its follower achieve specific goals. When we look at creation, we see that the Lord had a pattern for everything He wanted to do on earth. For us to continue the work God began in Genesis, it's so important to discover His pattern for specific callings or responsibilities.

Patterns are a blueprint developed and left behind for others to follow in order to reach the same goal. God established a specific pattern in everything He created. His divine pattern reveals His glorious purpose for us to follow, and when we follow it, His glory is manifested. A display of God's glory is a sign of His approval for the pattern we are following. In Exodus, Moses did everything according to God's pattern. God told him, "Make this tabernacle and all its furnishings exactly like the pattern I will show you" (Exodus 25:9). Later, we see that "Moses finished the work. Then the cloud covered the tent of meeting, and the glory of the LORD filled the tabernacle" (Exodus 40:33–34).

Only when we build according to divine pattern does God's approval come. He sanctions His standard, not necessarily our activities. A divine pattern is required for the fullness of His glory or the fire of God to fall. A pattern shapes our purpose. In biblical context, God gives people patterns to build according to His eternal plan and purpose, to reflect His glory, majesty, greatness, splendor, magnificence, holiness, excellence, power, and infinite nature.

God, the Master Planner, has a true blueprint, His Word, that stands the test of time and circumstances. It is for every generation to follow. He examines everything we build according to His blueprint. After the earth was destroyed by the Great Flood, the Lord told Noah's descendants to spread out and fill the earth. But they said to each other, "Come, let us build ourselves a city, with a tower that reaches to the heavens, so that we may make a name for ourselves; otherwise, we will be scattered over the face of the whole earth" (Genesis 11:4). Their plan was contrary to God's pattern. They built with their own pattern, for their own purposes and desires. The Lord came down to see what they were building, and He scattered them by confusing their language. The principle of this story remains the same today. The Lord comes down to see not only what we build, but also what pattern we are using to build it and for whose glory.

Biblically, patterns inspired by the Holy Spirit include His presence, creation, salvation, holiness, and authority as Creator and King. God, who knows and sees all things in advance, gives us a pattern so we can build according to what's on His heart. That's how a standard of excellence is established in Kingdom work. When God asks us to build for His glory, He already has the pattern, resources, power, and authority for us so we can build according to His design.

> I am GOD, the only God you've had or ever will have—incomparable, irreplaceable—from the very beginning telling you what the ending will be, all along letting you in on what is going to happen, assuring you, "I'm in this for the long haul, I'll do exactly what I set out to do."
>
> Isaiah 46:9–10 MSG

A divine pattern is established so you can build with God. After all, He is the Creator, Master Builder, Savior, sustainer, and owner! He has a pattern for your personal life, your marriage and family, your spiritual ministry, and your business. Working with God's pattern enables us to lead nations, manage economic resources, and bring about societal transformation. The question isn't, *Who needs a divine pattern?* But rather, *How much of a divine pattern do we need in order to see the fullness of God's glory manifested on the earth for all humanity to see?*

The fulfillment of Isaiah's prophecy is realized when we follow God's blueprint: "And the glory of the LORD will be revealed, and all people will see it together. For the mouth of the LORD has spoken" (Isaiah 40:5).

In the beginning, God created all the patterns, and it is by His revelation that we can build and establish new systems. In order for scientists, physicists, inventors, developers, and human creators to discover new concepts for today's society, they must receive revelation. In this modern world, for example, when a new car design is created and developed, a prototype is built according to detailed specifications. This allows the new car design to be duplicated on the assembly line exactly as intended. The revelation of a pattern is key to the process.

God placed His revelations in position from the beginning. "I am the Alpha and the Omega, the First and the Last, the Beginning and the End" (Revelation 22:13). He waited for people like Isaiah, Noah, Moses, and many others to seek Him for divine patterns. Biblical principles have within them divine patterns that bring change and transformation. The fivefold ministry is anointed to establish the divine blueprint for God's patterns by hearing what the Holy Spirit is saying to the Church.

Raising a VIP Generation

The acronym VIP is known in many languages and cultures. VIP means a *Very Important Person* and frequently refers to a dignitary. The *Oxford Dictionary* definitions of a VIP include a famous or important person of note, a dignitary or celebrity, etc.[1] In the Kingdom of God, the fivefold ministry is called to raise a biblical VIP generation for the Kingdom army of God, with divine order and strategies, and with *Value*, *Identity*, and *Purpose* (VIP), as we talked about at the start of this chapter. They are to raise and equip individuals who are grounded in their faith on biblical truth and values. These VIP individuals will establish their identity on a true relationship with God through eternal covenant, and they will commit to living a life that reflects their divine purpose. These are people who know what they believe, who they are, and what they live for.

- *Value* is the expression of what we believe about God, His Word, and our relationship with Him. For a believer, life starts with believing in Christ Jesus and His words. Our faith

transforms our value system since it changes our mindset. Our values come from what we believe about God and the Bible since faith comes by hearing and believing the Word (see Romans 10:17). The real question is, *What do you believe?* That's the foundation of our value system, also known as culture. In this context, culture is a total way of life.

- *Identity* is defined by the *Oxford Dictionary* as "who or what somebody/something is."[2] For God's people, our identity is what distinguishes us from other people. We know who we are because of our relationship with Christ; we are children of God. The question *Who are you?* can only be answered in relationship to our Creator and Redeemer: "You are a chosen people, a royal priesthood, a holy nation, God's special possession, that you may declare the praises of him who called you out of darkness into his wonderful light" (1 Peter 2:9). In my view, there is no better and more powerful definition of our identity than this verse.

- *Purpose* is the reason for which something exists or is done or made or used with an intended result in mind. Purpose is the result of our determination to live for what we believe we are called and empowered to fulfill on earth for the glory of God as the result of our values and identity. Purpose means answering the question *What and whom do you live for?* Our purpose is to do everything for the glory of God because of what we believe and who we are.

Ephesians 4:12–13 (NKJV) makes it very clear that the fivefold ministry is called primarily to raise the VIP generation: "The equipping of the saints for the work of ministry, for the edifying of the body of Christ, till we all come to the unity of the faith and of the knowledge of the Son of God, to a perfect man, to the measure of the stature of the fullness of Christ." *Equipping* can be defined as providing people with the necessary items and training to prepare and empower them to achieve a special goal. In Greek, the word for equip, *katartizō*, has the connotation of restoring, putting in order, mending, making complete, training, and so forth.[3]

Apostles and prophets are given authority to lay the foundation and bring revelation of the Word for true and biblically based faith. They provide sound strategy and prophetic direction to build on solid faith. Ephesians 2:20 tells us that as God's household we are "built on the foundation of the apostles and prophets, with Christ Jesus himself as the chief cornerstone."

Evangelists are called to make the Gospel relevant to the VIP generation by helping establish their identity as children of God. Evangelists bring life, hope, passion, fire, and excitement about the truth and power of the Gospel.

Pastors demonstrate love and godly protection. Pastors have big, caring hearts for the well-being of the VIP generation, and they want to help them understand their calling and purpose.

Teachers bring revelation of God's Word to the VIP generation. Teachers are highly motivated to equip through discipling, edifying, encouraging, training, and correcting. They are greatly needed for excellence, improvement, and capacity building for the

VIP generation. They are gifted in making complex ideas easy to understand and practical for self-evaluation and ongoing progress.

The fivefold ministers are called to find, raise, and equip a VIP generation with *Value*, *Identity*, and *Purpose* to advance the Kingdom of God on earth. We who are part of this generation are ambassadors of the Kingdom of light and life.

QUESTIONS FOR ABIDING DEEPER

- Look again at the VIP circles illustration. As part of the VIP generation in our day, what kind of answers would you give to the questions *What do you believe? Who are you? What do you live for?*
- Is there a time in your life when you received a divine pattern from God to build something for His Kingdom? What did that look like?
- Do you identify with any of the roles in the fivefold ministry? Have you asked God if He would have you serve in one of these capacities?

10

BREAKING THE CYCLE OF DECEPTION

ALEMU BEEFTU

One who breaks open the way will go up before them; they will break through the gate and go out. Their king will pass through before them, the LORD at their head.

Micah 2:13

God is looking for someone to restore the glory of true freedom in Christ. Throughout human history, individuals, families, people groups, and nations have fought for freedom. We are created in the image of God for freedom; we desire true freedom. As much as our Creator wants us to walk in true inner liberty, the enemy of our soul always fights against our freedom. God, our deliverer, hears the cry of every generation for freedom physically, spiritually, economically, and socially. The external cry, in most cases, is the expression of an inner cry.

The Israelites cried out for physical and spiritual freedom. Despite the promises of spiritual freedom (through the covenant of God being their God) and physical freedom (through the Promised Land being for them and their descendants), they suffered in slavery for four hundred years. They cried out to God to set them free from the yoke of slavery and the spiritual darkness of idol worship. Their divine deliverer responded,

> I have seen how cruelly my people are being treated in Egypt; I have heard them cry out to be rescued from their slave drivers. I know all about their sufferings, and so I have come down to rescue them. . . . I have indeed heard the cry of my people, and I see how the Egyptians are oppressing them.
>
> Exodus 3:7–9 GNT

This is a vivid picture of our cry for freedom and God's ability to liberate us. God heard His people's cry, saw their suffering, and gave them their freedom. The full manifestation of this is in the incarnation of Jesus. "When He saw the throngs, He was moved with pity and sympathy for them, because they were bewildered (harassed and distressed and dejected and helpless), like sheep without a shepherd" (Matthew 9:36 AMPC). That's why the Word came to dwell among us—for lasting freedom:

> The Spirit of the Lord [is] upon Me, because He has anointed Me [the Anointed One, the Messiah] to preach the good news (the Gospel) to the poor; He has sent Me to announce release to the captives and recovery of sight to the blind, to send forth as delivered those who are oppressed [who are downtrodden, bruised, crushed, and broken down by calamity].
>
> Luke 4:18 AMPC

The Cycle of Deception

One of the effective weapons the enemy has used in every generation is deception. In my opinion, any act of causing someone to believe or accept as true what is not is deception. This strategy started in the Garden. From Genesis 3 throughout the Bible, deception is used in different forms. In this context, deception may include lying, cheating, denying, or deceiving someone in order to mislead.

The enemy's goal is to distort God's original intent or purpose. The core of deception is to change the value or worth of something by replacing it with what isn't true, or with something temporary and less valuable, by appealing to human pleasure, desire, or ego. Using his evil strategy, the enemy's goal is to take us out of our fellowship, blessings, fulfillment, and any place where we are effective in the Kingdom. The enemy wants to put us into a cycle of deception. Satan used the same strategy when he deceived Eve:

> Then the serpent said to the woman, "You will not surely die. For God knows that in the day you eat of it your eyes will be opened, and you will be like God, knowing good and evil."
>
> So when the woman saw that the tree was good for food, that it was pleasant to the eyes, and a tree desirable to make one wise, she took of its fruit and ate. She also gave to her husband with her, and he ate.
>
> Genesis 3:4–6 NKJV

Satan's strategy included three distinct deceptions that we will examine one at a time. First, he made the word of the Lord seem false. Second, he made it seem as if there are no consequences to going our own way. Third, he gave false hope that led to doubting God's plan.

The First Deception

"You will not surely die." Satan made the word of the Lord seem false. Throughout human history, the enemy has used this deception.

Once a person rejects the word of the Lord, nothing is left, since everything God has for us is in His written Word. I once heard a pastor share a story from the pulpit that illustrated this point very well:

Once there was an American father with one child. The boy had grown up with good manners and a good education. His father promised him a reward if he did well in his doctoral degree. The boy's desire was to receive the most expensive red sports car of his time. The father agreed.

In time the young man graduated with honors, without embarrassing his father. The father set up a big party for his son's graduation. Because they were both believers, the feast was accompanied by singing and the Word of God. Finally, the father told the audience about his son's well-being and presented his son with a beautiful gift. The gift was a Bible.

When the young man saw that the gift was a Bible, he was extremely upset. Saddened by the fact that his father hadn't given him the promised gift, he put the Bible on a table and left the house, never to see his father again.

Many years later, realizing that it was time for him to go to heaven, the father looked for his son thoroughly and succeeded in talking to him over the phone. He begged his son to come visit him one last time. After several conversations, his son accepted the offer and came to see his father. But by the time he arrived home, his father had already passed away.

The fact that he wasn't going to see his dad again on this earth greatly troubled and saddened the son. He looked up and saw the Bible his father had given him at his graduation. While he was turning the pages, something fell from the Bible. When he saw the fallen object, he realized it was the key to his dream car. Just because he had been upset to see that his father's gift was a Bible and hadn't looked inside it, he had spent many years without enjoying his father's fellowship and without using his precious gift, which had been kept in the Bible.

The key to everything we need and want is in the eternal truth of the Word of God. We overcome deception by opening the Word of God.

The Second Deception

There will be "no consequences," and you will not die. Satan implies that nothing negative will happen to you if you choose to go your own way. In fact, it's better for you, he suggests, since you will gain knowledge. We start believing this deception and enter a snare of the enemy. Once a person enters this cycle of deception, the desire of knowing and experiencing new things becomes stronger. That's why the enemy told Eve their eyes would be opened and they would know good and evil. He appealed to their human value system: good for food, pleasing to the eyes, and desirable for gaining wisdom. James said about this, "But each person is tempted when they are dragged away by their own evil desire and enticed. Then, after desire has conceived, it gives birth to sin; and sin, when it is full-grown, gives birth to death" (James 1:14–15).

The Third Deception

"You will be like God." The greatest deception gives you false hope that leads you to doubt God's plan. When the enemy speaks, he doesn't reveal the truth since he doesn't have any truth in him; he is the father of lies and deception, and deception is the currency of the kingdom of darkness. He appeals to your human desire and ego. The cycle of deception is accepting or believing darkness as light and light as darkness. Adam and Eve were created in God's image, and they had God's breath in them. They wanted to be like God, but it was a false hope the enemy gave them. They didn't become like God. Instead, they were separated from God. Paul addressed this issue:

> But I am afraid that just as Eve was deceived by the serpent's cunning, your minds may somehow be led astray from your sincere and pure devotion to Christ. . . . And no wonder, for Satan himself

masquerades as an angel of light. It is not surprising, then, if his servants also masquerade as servants of righteousness.

2 Corinthians 11:3, 14–15

Nullifying the Word by convincing individuals that they have no personal responsibility for their actions is the basis of this deception.

Breakout for Breakthrough

The deception cycle starts with an urge to discover and know. Once Eve saw the fruit of the forbidden tree again, her desire to taste it grew. That led her into a craving for pleasure and the forbidden fruit. At this stage, the enemy uses visual sight, making things "pleasing to the eye" to create stronger cravings, and then the lust of the flesh starts exerting control. Such a convincing attraction leads to action: "She took of its fruit and ate. She also gave to her husband with her, and he ate" (Genesis 3:6 NKJV).

After the action, the nature of the deception becomes exposed. That desire ends in death, not in delight and enjoyment. Adam and Eve didn't become like God, but were separated from God. They were naked and filled with shame. That opened the door for the curse to enter their lives.

Jesus came to break the deception cycle in exchange for freedom and blessings. This causes a true breakout from the enemy's trap for those who call upon His name. "The reason the Son of God appeared was to destroy the devil's work" (1 John 3:8). Jesus is our deliverer, sent by the Father for this very reason. With David, we can rejoice in our deliverance by singing this song of freedom: "We have escaped like a bird from the fowler's snare; the snare has been broken, and we have escaped. Our help is in the name of the LORD, the Maker of heaven and earth" (Psalm 124:7–8).

The Word of the Lord declares freedom in Christ Jesus, by the power of the Holy Spirit, and by the authority of the Word:

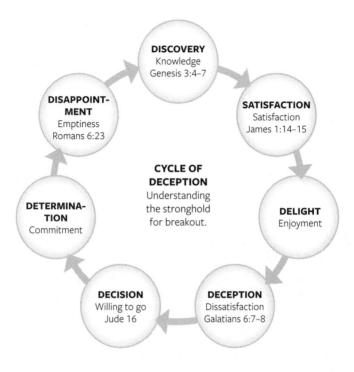

So if the Son sets you free, you will be free indeed (John 8:36).

Where the Spirit of the Lord is, there is freedom (2 Corinthians 3:17).

Then you will know the truth, and the truth will set you free (John 8:32).

These are our weapons to use to shatter strongholds and break out from the cycle of deception. The Word of the Lord is described this way:

The weapons we fight with are not the weapons of the world. On the contrary, *they have divine power to demolish strongholds.* We demolish arguments and every pretension that sets itself up against the knowledge of God, and we take captive every thought to make it obedient to Christ.

2 Corinthians 10:4–5, emphasis added

The way for true breakout is to follow the breaker of every deception and chain, the Lord Jesus Christ. He is the only one who replaces the cycle of deception in our lives with a cycle of victory as children of God. Jesus didn't come only to deliver us from the traps of life; He also came to lead us into a life of freedom as we follow Him: "The Breaker [the Messiah] will go up before them. They will break through, pass in through the gate and go out through it, and their King will pass on before them, the Lord at their head" (Micah 2:13 AMPC).

The life of breakout for breakthrough means reversing the cycle of deception for lasting, true freedom through the Lord Jesus. "To him who loves us and has freed us from our sins by his blood, and has made us to be a kingdom and priests to serve his God and Father—to him be glory and power for ever and ever! Amen" (Revelation 1:5–6). That "Amen" releases the power of Jesus' blood, the anointing of the Holy Spirit, and the power of the Gospel of our salvation to transform our mindset. It places us in a cycle of glorious freedom. Let's look at this healthy cycle that includes *discovery, desire, delight, decision, determination,* and *destiny.*

Discovery

God placed in us a desire to know. That pure knowledge and wisdom doesn't come from the tempter, but from above: "But the wisdom that comes from heaven is first of all pure; then peace-loving, considerate, submissive, full of mercy and good fruit, impartial and sincere" (James 3:17). Such wisdom honors God and draws us to Him. Paul prayed for the saints to have godly wisdom, and to have a deeper understanding and fulfill their calling by the power of the Holy Spirit:

I keep asking that the God of our Lord Jesus Christ, the glorious Father, may give you the Spirit of wisdom and revelation, so that you may know him better. I pray also that the eyes of your heart may be enlightened in order that you may know the hope to which he has called you, the riches of his glorious inheritance in the saints, and his incomparably great power for us who believe. That power is like the working of his mighty strength.

Ephesians 1:17–19

Desire

When we are open to this spirit of understanding, revelation, and wisdom, our inner desires and sensitive insights change. We focus on our victory and eternal hope. "Since, then, you have been raised with Christ, set your hearts on things above, where Christ is seated at the right hand of God. Set your minds on things above, not on earthly things" (Colossians 3:1–2).

Delight

This heart change transforms our desires as well. "Delight yourself in the LORD and he will give you the desires of your heart" (Psalm 37:4). Like Moses, we start delighting in the will of the Lord, instead of the temporary pleasures of sin: "He chose to be mistreated along with the people of God rather than to enjoy the pleasures of sin for a short time" (Hebrews 11:25).

Decision

We overcome the enemy's temptation because of our breakout experience through the power of Jesus' blood. Then our decisions, like Daniel's, change so we can avoid whatever comes to defile our mind and spirit: "But Daniel resolved not to defile himself with the royal food and wine" (Daniel 1:8). When we walk daily with God in a life of prayer and worship, we overcome temptation. We protect our freedom. We live worthy of our freedom by counting the cost and making firm decisions, trusting the Lord for victory or a way out, like Daniel. Other times, we slow down and avoid, or even run away from, the enemy's snare he tries to place in our way: "Flee the evil desires of youth, and pursue righteousness, faith, love and peace, along with those who call on the Lord out of a pure heart" (2 Timothy 2:22). Pursuing these spiritual fruits is a sign of breakout for breakthrough.

Determination

Sincere decision leads to determination. This is an act of firmly deciding with resolve. This is a willingness to pay the price or face the consequences for standing on the truth. One of the signs of breakthrough is a willingness to live for the glory of God, whatever the price might be. That's what the cost of discipleship is all about. We carry the cross and follow Jesus daily by declaring in life and words that there is one God to worship, one Savior to believe in, one Father to love, one Holy Spirit to hear and obey, one baptism to receive, one Body of Christ, one Gospel to preach, one name to trust, one Lord to follow, one cross to carry, and one life to live to honor Him.

Destiny

Such determination will bring us to our prophetic destiny. That's what we have been created, saved, and anointed for. Destiny is about the preplanned will and desire of God for each person. That prophetic destiny is well defined in Romans 8:29–30:

> For those God foreknew he also predestined to be conformed to the likeness of his Son, that he might be the firstborn among many brothers. And those he predestined, he also called; those he called, he also justified; those he justified, he also glorified.

The call to be conformed into the image of Christ starts with a breakout for breakthrough that leads us into the discovery of who our God is as we follow Him with decision and determination, reaching our prophetic destiny and transforming into His image daily.

A Different Spirit

Breakthrough leads us to discover who we are in God. Our prophetic destiny starts with knowing who we are. This helps reveal who our God is. The knowledge of God leads us into discovering our new identity so we can walk in true spiritual freedom and authority.

Once someone experiences true spiritual transformation through the work of the Holy Spirit by breaking the cycle of deception, that person won't try to establish a personal kingdom on the pretense of advancing the Kingdom of God. Instead, that person follows the Lord wholeheartedly, with a different spirit, as Caleb did: "Because my servant Caleb has a different spirit and follows me wholeheartedly, I will bring him into the land he went to, and his descendants will inherit it" (Numbers 14:24).

QUESTIONS FOR ABIDING DEEPER

- Do you recognize some of the ways the enemy comes to deceive? Have you succumbed to some of those deceptions?
- Look again at the illustration of the "Breakout for Breakthrough" cycle. Where are you in this cycle?

11

VISION TO MAKE HISTORY

ALEMU BEEFTU

I was not disobedient to the vision from heaven.

Acts 26:19

God is always looking for a visionary who will restore the reflection of His glory and build according to His revealed patterns. In every generation, people attempt to do something new that hasn't yet been accomplished. These individuals are referred to as *history makers*. These are the people who create, make, or correct things for effectiveness and usefulness in an innovative way. It means stepping out to do what was never done before and facing the challenges that come with it.

In most cases, history makers change the course of history for the better by paying the price such change demands. God looks in every generation first for history makers, second for those who correct history (having the courage to right wrongs and rebuild), and third for those who would share history (by recording and relating it for future generations).

History makers have some identifiable character traits that make them different and effective in their generation. These traits include knowing and walking with God, and loving and obeying Him whole-heartedly. They also include having a long-term dream, a clear vision of God, focus, and determination. History makers are also driven by God and by a compelling desire to please Him, and driven by their compassion for a generation. They refuse to hurl blame, and they have true humility, meekness, serving hearts, peace of mind, and the joy of the Lord. Individuals with these character traits strongly believe in and live by the will of God, heart of God, mind of Christ, power of the Holy Spirit, and revelation of God's Word.

A Vision of God

Out of all the character traits just listed, a clear vision of God is the most important one. It's the foundation for all other godly charac-teristics. Every redeemed history maker starts with a true vision of who God is. History makers have the desire and ability to see a bigger picture and do something about it. Because of what they see, they don't settle for less, nor are they satisfied with temporary things. Their vision doesn't start with what's around them. They look for what's beyond their natural ability to see or observe. They see God in His greatness. They see what He sees in them and for them. They see the potential in others, and they see His eternal plan. They see the way the Lord sees things, and they operate with God's values.

The vision of history makers starts with seeing God, what He sees, the way He sees, and seeing the future and Kingdom through His eyes. The foundation of their vision is their relationship with Him. It's not about them or their ability, but about their God and His greatness, despite what they might feel about themselves or others. They start their journey with a holy reverence of God. Let's look at some biblical examples of history makers—Moses, Isaiah, Elijah, and the apostle John.

Moses

Moses started his history-making journey by covering his face in God's presence: "Then He said, 'I am the God of your father, the God of Abraham, the God of Isaac and the God of Jacob.' At this, Moses hid his face, because he was afraid to look at God" (Exodus 3:6). Yet Moses became one of the most powerful and effective biblical characters in making and correcting history, breaking the yoke of four hundred years of slavery.

The martyr Stephen stated, "Moses was educated in all the wisdom of the Egyptians and was powerful in speech and action" (Acts 7:22). Moses became a history maker by setting the people of God free through mighty signs and wonders. He didn't just have a glimpse of a vision of God; he dwelt in God's presence, in the glory zone. He spoke with God face-to-face. He started with a vision of God in the fire, and with hearing God's voice coming out of the fire. He kept that vision of God until the end.

No wonder Moses acknowledged the attributes of God as a holy, consuming fire and said that He was a jealous God. Because Moses had this vision of God, his prayer, even at an old age, was about the favor, presence, and glory of God. God answered his prayer by preparing a special place for Moses near Him.

Isaiah

The prophet Isaiah's destiny manifested the year King Uzziah died. Isaiah saw a vision of God, but he didn't feel that he was walking in holiness as he should when he saw the Lord. Yet even that feeling of unworthiness didn't stop him from seeing God in His majesty and greatness: "In the year that King Uzziah died, I saw the Lord, high and exalted, seated on a throne; and the train of his robe filled the temple" (Isaiah 6:1). The death of King Uzziah didn't distort or limit

Isaiah's vision of the greatness of God. Because of God's holiness, Isaiah cried out for His cleansing mercy.

Elijah

History makers don't take God's holiness lightly; neither do they get used to it. That's one of the signs of true humility. Like Moses, Elijah covered his face in God's presence: "The LORD said, 'Go out and stand on the mountain in the presence of the LORD, for the LORD is about to pass by.' . . . When Elijah heard it, he pulled his cloak over his face and went out and stood at the mouth of the cave" (1 Kings 19:11, 13).

Elijah was dedicated to God's cause, and he was driven by his zeal for God's glory. Elijah prayed that the rain would stop until the Israelites recognized God as the true and only provider and turned their hearts to Him. God not only heard him; He also gave him authority to stop the rain by closing the heavens for three and a half years.

Elijah repaired the altar of God and prayed for fire. The Lord answered him with fire that consumed the altar, sacrifice, stone, dirt, and water. He prayed for rain again, and the Lord sent the rain as He put His hand upon him. Elijah was the history maker who destroyed the idol worshipers, turned the hearts of the nation to God, restored the covenant relationship, and repaired the altar of God, the altar of Abraham, Isaac, and Jacob.

The apostle John

John saw the Lord in the spirit during his exile and suffering on Patmos. As a determined history maker, he rose above his circumstances. In the middle of his suffering, he heard the voice of his Lord and turned around to see the Lord Jesus in the middle of the seven churches: "When I saw him, I fell at his feet and as though dead. Then he placed his right hand on me" (Revelation 1:17).

John would reveal the mysteries of the heavens and the future of earth because of his vision. However, he didn't stop with that one experience. He followed God's mandate and corrected the seven churches. He was told, "Write, therefore, what you have seen, what is now and what will take place later" (Revelation 1:19). After what John saw, heard, and received, he brought needed correction to the churches.

A Higher Vision

History makers don't stop with an initial vision; they move into a higher vision and understanding, just like the apostle John. After his amazing vision, he brought needed correction, and then he responded to the calling to come higher: "The voice I had first heard speaking to me like a trumpet said, 'Come up here, and I will show you what must take place after this.' At once I was in the Spirit, and there before me was a throne in heaven with someone sitting on it" (Revelation 4:1–2).

Note that the invitation was for John to see what he hadn't seen before. He was to see a new revelation about what was yet to come. Greater vision! Vision is seeing what's not here yet. That, and what follows in this list, are key for history makers:

- First, John heard the same voice that had called him before. History makers may receive a clear call of God at the beginning, and the same voice continues calling them to a higher, deeper relationship with Him.
- Second, there was an open door in heaven, meaning God was ready to welcome John and show him more. Since the door was open in heaven, no one could shut it.
- Third, John was in the Spirit. Every true history maker needs to walk in the sevenfold manifestation of the Spirit of God that was on the Lord Jesus Christ: "The *Spirit of the* Lord will rest on him—the *Spirit of wisdom* and of

understanding, the *Spirit of counsel* and of *might,* the *Spirit of the knowledge* and *fear of the* LORD" (Isaiah 11:2, emphasis added). Nothing is more important for history makers than to understand and be filled with these manifestations and walk in them daily.

- Fourth, John was ushered into the throne room of the King of kings and Lord of lords. This is like Isaiah's vision. Once history makers see the Lord God Almighty on His throne, they are only able to live for Him. The throne room also teaches history makers the protocol of the King and His Kingdom. Isaiah made reference to this later in his writing: "Your eyes will see the King in His beauty; [your eyes] will behold a land of wide distances that stretches afar" (Isaiah 33:17 AMPC).

The vision of history makers starts with the beauty and majesty of the King. The vision of a promised land or our calling comes only after the beauty and greatness of our King is revealed. History makers start with God, and their vision always takes them into the throne room, combining authority and worship. That was where King Uzziah missed it. Because of his position and earthly authority, he felt he was authorized to do whatever he wanted. He didn't honor the God who made him powerful. Once powerful, he stopped seeking the Lord and entered the Temple to make sacrifices from his proud heart (see 2 Chronicles 26:16).

John had never before experienced just how much more highly exalted God's throne is above any human throne. It displayed the absolute authority of God! That is the throne Isaiah saw the year King Uzziah died. All effective visions come after seeing the King on His throne. Isaiah had a new understanding of his calling after he saw the Lord on His throne in the temple.

It is amazing to see the combination of the throne room and the temple worship. The temple is a place of the manifested presence of God. It is a place of His dwelling, of His footstool. That is why John was taken into the throne room, where he saw the One who sat on the throne, and where he heard, just like Isaiah, the sound of worship:

> In the center, around the throne, were four living creatures, and they were covered with eyes, in front and in back. . . . Each of the four living creatures had six wings and was covered with eyes all around, even under its wings. Day and night they never stop saying,
>
>> Holy, holy, holy
>> is the Lord God Almighty,
>> who was, and is, and is to come.
>
> Revelation 4:6–8

"What Do You See?"

History makers work with God's vision, meaning it's a vision initiated by God that focuses on Him. He gives vision and then asks what we see, to make sure our vision aligns with His. Old Testament prophets were referred to as *seers*. They were called to see by the Spirit of God what others couldn't. Their mandates included giving directions, revealing the mysteries of heaven, putting into human language what they saw by the Spirit, declaring God's will and purpose about the future, bringing warnings as watchmen, and preparing the people for God's plans and blessings by calling them to repentance. These prophets or seers revealed God's will as they released His word for correction, direction, and confirmation.

These ancient prophets were the best history makers, since they knew the heart of God. For that reason, the Lord asked them, "What do you see?" The prophets Amos and Zechariah each were asked twice. Jeremiah was asked three times, because of his calling to build, plant, and correct history. He uprooted, tore down, and overthrew nations and kingdoms that worked against God's plan (see Jeremiah

1:11, 13; 24:3). Jeremiah's correct vision gave the Lord an open door to fulfill His word.

The Lord not only asked these prophets (seers) what they were seeing, but He also told Habakkuk to write his vision for others to see and read as a witness to God's faithfulness. Every vision from God has its appointed time to be fulfilled; it is never delayed.

Furthermore, the vision God gives is bigger than feelings and struggles. Because of his great vision and God's promises, Jeremiah withstood persecution from his people. One of the greatest gifts God gives history makers, along with a calling and clear vision, is a promise of victory. He told Jeremiah the nation would fight against him, but would not be able to overcome him, because of God's presence within him.

The authority and power of history makers comes from God's presence to protect and rescue them, and to accomplish His will through them. That was the assurance God gave all His servants throughout history. When Moses told Him that his assignment was too big and he couldn't do it, God's answer was simple and direct: *I will be with you*. When God called Joshua to take the Israelites into the Promised Land by destroying the current inhabitants, He promised, "No one will be able to stand up against you all the days of your life. As I was with Moses, so I will be with you; I will never leave you nor forsake you" (Joshua 1:5). There is no greater history maker than Joshua. He didn't lose God's promises of victory, and God's presence never left.

Requirements for History Makers

God has certain requirements for His history makers. They are required to:

- Have a clear vision or see correctly. "The LORD said to me, 'You have seen correctly, for I am watching to see that my word is fulfilled'" (Jeremiah 1:12).

- Rest and be secure in His presence. "So I will be with you; I will never leave you nor forsake you" (Joshua 1:5).
- Meditate on His Word. "Keep this Book of the Law always on your lips; meditate on it day and night" (Joshua 1:8).
- Write down the vision. "Write the vision and engrave it so plainly upon tablets that everyone who passes may [be able to] read [it easily and quickly] as he hastens by" (Habakkuk 2:2 AMPC).
- Walk by faith. "But the righteous person will live by his faithfulness" (Habakkuk 2:4).
- Worship continually. "A prayer of Habakkuk the prophet, set to wild, enthusiastic, and triumphal music" (Habakkuk 3:1 AMPC).
- Walk in the fear of God. "O Lord, I have heard the report of You and was afraid" (Habakkuk 3:2 AMPC).
- Pray for the move of God and renewal. "O Lord, revive Your work in the midst of the years, in the midst of the years make [Yourself] known! In wrath [earnestly] remember love, pity, and mercy" (Habakkuk 3:2 AMPC).

History makers are visionaries. Their vision starts with God and moves to purpose and life assignments. They start with a vision and live for the vision, despite the potential challenges.

The apostle Paul started his history-making journey with a divine encounter (see Acts 9). When he saw the Lord Jesus, his first question was, "Who are you, Lord?" After the Lord Jesus told him, Paul's second question was, "What would You have me do?" To receive an answer for that question, he was told to go to the city of Damascus. In the city, after Paul had fasted and sought the Lord for three days, the Lord sent Ananias to him. Ananias prayed and laid hands on Paul, and Paul received his sight again. The old scales fell from his eyes, and he was filled with the Holy Spirit. As a history maker, Paul had the following traits and experiences:

- First, he had an encounter with the Lord Jesus.
- Second, he learned to wait upon the Lord and seek Him before taking action.
- Third, he learned to submit to the authority of another apostle.
- Fourth, he received a new vision for the rest of his ministry life.
- Fifth, he received the power of the Holy Spirit to become a history maker.
- Sixth, he became the carrier of the name of the Lord, which was the crucial aspect of his ministry.
- Seventh, he received the core of his calling, "To know his will and to see the Righteous One and to hear words from his mouth" (Acts 22:14).
- Eighth, he had total obedience to the vision. Paul said, "I was not disobedient to the vision from heaven" (Acts 26:19).
- Ninth, he moved into a greater vision when he "was caught up to paradise and heard inexpressible things, things that no one is permitted to tell" (2 Corinthians 12:4).
- Tenth, he ran the race with faithfulness and focus to the end.

These points about Paul summarize the true calling, life, and vision of effective history makers whom the Lord is looking for in this generation.

QUESTIONS FOR ABIDING DEEPER

- Who is a history maker who inspires you? What grips you the most about his or her life and vision?
- How do you think God's vision differs from the vision of our culture? What is God's ultimate goal?

12

DREAM TO MAKE HISTORY

Alemu Beeftu

Joseph had a dream, and when he told it to his brothers, they hated him all the more.

Genesis 37:5

God is looking for someone to dream His dream and restore the revelation of His glory by making history. History makers are dreamers. Since they see God and what He sees, their dream is God's dream.

On the Day of Pentecost, the Church was mandated to have vision, dream God's dream, and prophesy. God's Word and the Holy Spirit equipped the Church to become the last history maker on earth. That's the reason why Jesus built His Church so strong that the gates of hell cannot overcome it. He knew true history makers with visions, dreams, and the Kingdom message would face serious challenges from the forces of darkness.

Throughout history, the Church Jesus has been building has been persecuted. Yet the call of the Church as the last history maker in this world is to raise young visionaries, and to encourage and support dreamers to advance the Kingdom's work, despite the challenges.

Mission, Vision, and Dreams

By definition, a *dream* is a state of mind in which images, thoughts, and impressions pass through the mind of a person who is sleeping. But the root of the Hebrew word for *dream* means "to be made healthy," or "to recover."[1] That meaning still applies to dreams that produce images, thoughts, and impressions.

God uses dreams to guide us to the strength and health available by being obedient to His will. On that basis, dreams can transform into aspirations and hope. Not everything we call a dream is given by God. However, God often generates and uses the experience we know as dreams for His purposes.

The first type of dream I want to talk about is given to individuals as a means of communication from God, through the Holy Spirit. God sometimes communicates in this way by sending angels in a dream. Other times, God reveals Himself in dreams. As a means of communication from God, such dreams are not limited to history makers in Kingdom work. God also gives such dreams to others to reveal His will. The interpretation is given to people who know the Lord and have the specific gift of interpretation from God. This first type of dream is the more common type that God uses to complete His will and purpose.

The second type of dream is the prophetic or revelatory dream. Prophetic in nature and meaning, these dreams are given by the Holy Spirit to reveal God's heart. God uses prophetic dreams to show what's coming. For example, Joseph had dreams about his calling and what would happen in his life (see Genesis 37). Daniel dreamed of future events (see Daniel 7). Joseph and Daniel were not only dreamers; they were also gifted in interpreting dreams.

There are many prophetic dreams in the Bible. Our purpose or scope is not to deal with prophetic dreams here, however. We are focusing on dreams to describe "big thinking" for the sake of God's calling on history makers. Clearly, there is a connection between "big thinking" that is driven by God and the dreams He sends. Dreams from God expand the thinking, and therefore the greater impact, of history makers.

Along with dreams, there is the mission and vision of history makers. Mission enables them to define their call with authority. Vision gives them a basis for the core values that form their goals or strategic direction. Vision also gives them the passion to push through a process of ongoing improvement as they see things through God's eyes. It is important for history makers to understand the relationship between these three concepts:

- *Mission*—existence, defining what the call is
- *Vision*—excellence, determining what to improve
- *Dreams*—expansion, developing the territory for greater results

Dreams Push the Boundaries

Dreaming means thinking with a renewed mind to overcome limitations. Dreams encourage us to reach higher and wider to expand our field of impact as we obey God's will and carry out His purpose. Dreams push the boundaries for a greater result because of His power within us.

> Now to Him Who, by (in consequence of) the [action of His] power that is at work within us, is able to [carry out His purpose and] do superabundantly, far over and above all that we [dare] ask or think [infinitely beyond our highest prayers, desires, thoughts, hopes, or dreams].
>
> Ephesians 3:20 AMPC

Dreams help us overcome not only external limitations, but also internal limitations and hindrances. Maturity in the faith and in our spiritual life encourages us to dream. Perhaps that is one reason Acts 2:17 declares, "Your old men will dream dreams." Dreaming requires maturity because it focuses far beyond short-term successes and benefits. Having a dream means seeing the big picture beyond any boundary demarcation. A dream is bigger than life.

Having a dream means touching the generations still to come. When Martin Luther King Jr. declared, "I have a dream," he wasn't talking about personal, temporary gain. As a history maker, he was addressing the new generation of Americans who could create history by refusing to judge themselves and others "on the color of their skin," instead considering "the content of their character." Dr. King's dream was founded on a solid mission, a well-defined purpose of existence. His clear vision and lasting biblical values still bring hope and victory to the generations who followed him. His dream was far-reaching in its impact.

True dreamers are very important to ministry, businesses, and even nations. The power of dreams and their far-reaching implications to make a difference mean that dreamers ought to be people of character, with proven maturity. This is for the sake of the dreamer, as well as for those the dreamer impacts. Because of their prophetic nature, dreamers are not well understood in society. To be a good dreamer, a person must have a solid foundation that doesn't shake easily.

The Price of Dreaming God's Dreams

Another reason why maturity is a prerequisite for dreamers is the price history makers often pay. At times, the price is too high, as shown through many examples both in history and the Bible. Martin Luther King Jr. paid with his life for having a dream. That may sound too extreme, but the truth is that every serious dreamer should be willing to pay the price for his or her dream. In fact, if a dreamer isn't mature enough to calculate the price, that person is probably not worthy to have a dream.

Joseph had a dream and told his brothers, "Listen to this dream I had" (Genesis 37:6). Because of his dream, Joseph paid the price of emotional and physical alienation from his family. Still, he handled every challenge that came with being a dreamer with maturity and purpose of destiny. Some of the price Joseph paid is applicable to history makers still today. The costs included facing hatred, jealousy, ridicule, personal attacks, temptations, and testing by the Word of God. Let's look at each of these briefly.

Hatred

Joseph's brothers hated him because of his dream. "When he told it to his brothers, they hated him all the more" (Genesis 37:5). It's a hard thing when you're hated just because of your dream. It's more difficult when close family members or formerly faithful friends are among those who hate you. This hatred is partially the result of people misunderstanding both the dreamer and the dream. But it still hurts. Individuals who would like to be popular don't dare to dream; instead, they blame everyone else for the problems they see.

Jealousy

Authentic dreams often draw or stir up jealousy. That's what happened to Joseph when his brothers heard his dream. "His brothers were jealous of him" (Genesis 37:11). As a dreamer, Joseph had the maturity at a young age to handle this with love. Maturity isn't necessarily related to age, but to character. Anyone who desires to make a difference ought to have this character trait.

Ridicule

When jealousy didn't shake Joseph, his brothers came up with another weapon of attack. They started mocking him. They laughed at his dream. "Do you intend to reign over us? Will you actually rule us? . . . Here comes that dreamer!" (Genesis 37:8, 19). The main goal of the enemy at this point was to discourage Joseph by using his own brothers. In a leader's early stages of dreaming, discouragement from close friends, colleagues, or family members is often the most effective weapon the enemy has.

Personal Attacks

People who are easily threatened usually attack a dream. If that doesn't work, they attack the dreamer or visionary. When their attacks on Joseph's dream had no effect, Joseph's brothers turned their assaults on Joseph himself. First, they stripped off his robe and destroyed it. Joseph's ornamental clothing was a sign of what he would be in the future, a visible reminder of his dream for his brothers (see Genesis 37:18–20, 23–24, 31).

The good news is that the power of a dream doesn't depend on external appearances and signs. The power of a dream reflects the inner strengths or character of the dreamer. Joseph's brothers took his clothes, but they weren't able to take his dream. The lesson we learn from Joseph is that he didn't give up on his dream because of the challenges he faced on the journey toward fulfilling his destiny.

Joseph's brothers continued their attacks by throwing him into a cistern, intending to kill him. Finally, they sold Joseph into slavery instead, and he was taken to Egypt. He went through a very painful process, but it was the price of being a dreamer and history maker. Every difficult step he took brought him closer to fulfilling his dream. When a dreamer is determined to pay the necessary price for his or her dream and focuses on the result, everything works out for good. As Joseph said to his brothers, "You intended to harm me, but God intended it for good to accomplish what is now being done, the saving of many lives" (Genesis 50:20).

Temptations

If the enemy can't bring down a dreamer through emotional and personal attacks, he comes to tempt the dreamer through desire and need. In Joseph's case, temptation came through the lonely wife of his master. "After a while his master's wife took notice of Joseph and said, 'Come to bed with me!'" (Genesis 39:7).

Temptation came to Joseph robed in love and admiration. This is one of the most difficult tests—a true test of character and faithfulness. The hard part is not only resisting the temptation, but also accepting the false accusation and character assassination that often come with rejecting temptation. Potiphar's wife was so outraged by Joseph's repeated refusal of her advances that she accused him of attempted rape (see Genesis 39:13–19). In addition to being falsely accused, Joseph lost his position and suffered in prison for some time. Scripture says, "They bruised his feet with shackles, his neck was put in irons" (Psalm 105:18). Yet as Joseph's dream came to fruition, the Lord changed the bruises on his feet into authority: "Then Pharaoh said to Joseph, 'I am Pharaoh, but without your word no one will lift hand or foot in all Egypt'" (Genesis 41:44).

Testing by the Word of God

Sometimes challenges to a history maker come by way of other people or unfriendly circumstances. But God's Word also challenges dreamers and their dreams. As a dreamer, Joseph still had to pass the test of the word of God: "Until the time came to fulfill his dreams, the LORD tested Joseph's character" (Psalm 105:19 NLT).

Every dreamer who would like to accomplish great things has to pass the character test. God takes us through the necessary process to develop our character as history makers. The call of God doesn't lead us into instant maturity. Instead, it allows Him to mold and make us into leaders through the process of character building.

Making Is a Process

God's plan is to make us dreamers and leaders with character that reflects His image. Notice that Jesus said to the disciples, "Follow Me, and I will make you fishers of men" (Matthew 4:19 NKJV). He didn't say, "You will be . . ." Instead, He said, "I will make you . . ."

Making is a process, and the character-building process isn't always pleasant. Yet this process is crucial to achieving a quality outcome. In order for a dreamer to completely fulfill the purpose of God, the character-building process is as necessary as the fulfillment of the dream.

In ancient Ethiopia, gold was mined. After it was excavated, the gold was ready for purification, making it ready for market. The miners placed a large metal plate with holes over a raging fire. After the plate became hot, they dumped the gold and dirt onto the plate. They increased the intensity of the fire's flame for several days, until the dirt melted off. After a few more days, the miners stopped the fire. When the gold cooled completely, the supervisor made a purity check. If he could clearly see his image in the gold, like a good mirror, the gold was pure enough to take to market. But if his image was distorted or cloudy, the purification process was repeated.

Joseph went through the character-building process without complaining about his brothers or Potiphar's wife. History makers don't complain. Because of this, Joseph not only had a dream, but also experienced the manifested presence of God, and others noticed this in him. Potiphar noticed God's presence with Joseph, even though Joseph didn't say anything about it: "The LORD was with Joseph so that he prospered, and he lived in the house of his Egyptian master" (Genesis 39:2). The keeper of Joseph's prison responded to God's presence with Joseph:

> But the LORD was with Joseph and showed him mercy, and He gave him favor in the sight of the keeper of the prison. . . . The keeper of

the prison did not look into anything that was under Joseph's author-ity, because the LORD was with him; and whatever he did, the LORD made it prosper.

Genesis 39:21, 23 NKJV

Pharaoh also testified to God's presence with Joseph: "And Pharaoh said to his servants, 'Can we find such a one as this, a man in whom is the Spirit of God?'" (Genesis 41:38 NKJV). Joseph's example dem-onstrates that, more than anything else, the success of a dreamer is proven through the approval and presence of God, which should be the core issue in the life of history makers.

Used by God in the Process

God uses dreamers on their journeys. When we are sensitive to His will and purpose, He uses us every day as we make our way toward our dreams and destiny. God didn't wait until Joseph became governor of Egypt to show him great favor. Joseph was favored by Jacob, his father, by Potiphar, his master, by his prison keeper, and by Pharaoh himself, all because of God.

Joseph became a great blessing to many while he was waiting for his own dream to become a reality. He went on to become a blessing to his brothers after they rejected him and sold him into slavery. He became a great blessing to Potiphar and his household (including Potiphar's wife) due to God giving Joseph management skills: "From the time he put him in charge of his household and of all that he owned, the LORD blessed the household of the Egyptian because of Joseph. The blessing of the LORD was on everything Potiphar had, both in the house and in the field" (Genesis 39:5).

While in prison, Joseph became a problem solver and a source of encouragement to the prison keeper and the other prisoners. When Joseph saw a couple of other prisoners who were upset one morning, he asked them about it:

When Joseph came to them the next morning, he saw that they were dejected. So he asked Pharaoh's officials who were in custody with him in his master's house, "Why do you look so sad today?"

"We both had dreams," they answered, "but there is no one to interpret them."

Then Joseph said to them, "Do not interpretations belong to God? Tell me your dreams."

Genesis 40:6–8

The powerful phrase in this passage is *Tell me your dreams*. Joseph was still waiting for his own dreams to come to pass, but that didn't stop him from being used by God to interpret the dreams of others. This is the kind of character every history maker should exhibit in his or her life. Everyone who has a calling to become a history maker and a dreamer for a ministry or organization ought to ask his or her followers about their dreams. If you are a dreamer, don't wait until you fully understand your own dream before you help others with their dreams. God is ready to use you, even if you feel imprisoned now.

God gives dreamers a taste of success while on the journey to their destiny, just as He did with Joseph in the house of Potiphar: "The LORD was with Joseph, so he succeeded in everything he did" (Genesis 39:2 NLT). Joseph was used by God to accomplish His will in the process. Success for Joseph included the fulfillment of his dream. The young outcast from a shepherd's large family became the interpreter of Pharaoh's dreams and eventually the second-in-command ruler of Egypt. All the details of his long-held dream of being an honored provider for both his family and the nations finally came true.

To fulfill God's purpose as history makers, we must have a solid mission, a clear vision, and a big dream. Joseph became a very successful leader because he combined these three. Along with his dreams, Joseph's mission can be defined as a call to save lives: "God intended it for good to accomplish what is now being done, the saving of many lives" (Genesis 50:20). Joseph's vision was using his gift to serve others wherever he found himself, whether in Potiphar's house, a prison, or Pharaoh's court.

Our mission establishes our identity, which in turn defines a clearer purpose for our lives. This enables us to know and embrace the call of God. On the other hand, our vision, drawing its strength from clear purpose, empowers us to develop our God-given potential to glorify the Lord by giving our best. Having focus and core values provides a strong foundation and a long-term vision to dream big.

A big-thinking dream expands your territory of influence and impact. Such a dream affirms your calling and develops your gifts with a clearer vision. The effectiveness of a dreamer is proven through the ability to think with a sound mind, and to show strong character and clear vision: "As he [any person] thinks in his heart, so is he" (Proverbs 23:7 NKJV).

QUESTIONS FOR ABIDING DEEPER

- What is a dream God has placed on your heart? How has it prompted you to be more "big thinking"?
- Have you had to go through a refining process of character building to prepare for that dream to become a reality? What has that involved?
- Have you had to pay a price for your dream? How did God work it out for the good?

13

CORRECTING HISTORY

Alemu Beeftu

Your people will rebuild the ancient ruins and will raise up the age-old foundations; you will be called Repairer of Broken Walls, Restorer of Streets with Dwellings.

Isaiah 58:12

God is looking for someone with the determination to restore the revelation of His glory. Becoming a history maker means correcting what went wrong and building on a right or solid foundation. One of the traits of history makers is that they don't waste their time blaming others for what went wrong. They believe the Word, and they operate on it. The Lord doesn't want us to live in the past and lose our hope for the future. History makers learn from the past and live for the future, in obedience to the Word of the Lord.

"Forget the former things; do not dwell on the past. See, I am doing a new thing! Now it springs up; do you not perceive it? I am making a way in the wilderness and streams in the wasteland" (Isaiah 43:18–19). This passage starts with a command, "Forget." That means to purposefully lose the remembrance or memory of something, for the sake of what's coming. When we stop dwelling on the past, we can lift our eyes from where we are and see all the possibilities and promises of God. That doesn't mean denying what has happened; it means recognizing it and making it right. Then we are to lift our eyes from where we are and look into the future, just as Abraham was told: "Lift up your eyes from where you are and look north and south, east and west" (Genesis 13:14 NIV1984).

True history makers with a mission are grounded. Their vision enables them to see correctly, while their dream gives them the determination to pay the price. They take responsibility by remaining accountable. For them, making history and correcting history, along with shaping the future, cannot be separated. A vision of making history starts with a clear vision for correcting what went wrong and preparing the ground for a new, solid foundation. That's why Isaiah encouraged history makers to pay the price to rebuild, starting with a foundation that will last: "Your people will rebuild the ancient ruins and will raise up the age-old foundations; you will be called Repairer of Broken Walls, Restorer of Streets with Dwellings" (Isaiah 58:12).

Building something that lasts requires a solid foundation. Every true history maker starts with a solid foundation. The Lord Jesus referred to the importance of a foundation:

> Therefore everyone who hears these words of mine and puts them into practice is like *a wise man who built his house on the rock*. The rain came down, the streams rose, and the winds blew and beat against that house; yet it did not fall, because it *had its foundation on the rock*.
>
> Matthew 7:24–25, emphasis added

Here, Jesus makes reference to a foundation that is the Word of God and divine guidance. What is built on the Word withstands all three challenges that come against a building: rain (attacks from above), winds (challenges from the surrounding sides), and flood (hidden challenges that try to erode the foundation).

Zerubbabel, Joshua, and Nehemiah not only had a vision to rebuild on the right foundation, but they also did it without accusing those who went before them. Their vision was to bring back once again the presence, glory, worship, and blessings of God to their nation. Their vision was to bring back hope by correcting historical disobedience and the neglect of the things of the Lord.

History makers focus on the future by envisioning what could be again. They correct history, restoring it back to God's plan and purpose, returning to His original design and purpose. That's why it's called rebuilding the old foundation. They start with God and do it for God.

History makers are committed to work with God by walking with Him. They seek God first, correcting and rebuilding their relationship with Him, knowing His heart and receiving forgiveness and divine strategy on how to correct and rebuild. When Nehemiah heard about the condition of Jerusalem's wall, he started with a prayer of confession and repentance: "When I heard these things, I sat down and wept" (Nehemiah 1:4). History makers are driven not only by passion and commitment to rebuild, but also by compassion and care for the glory of God's name.

Nehemiah received special favor, permission, time to build, resources, and strategy. Most of all, the gracious hand of the Lord came upon him to rebuild, and to have powerful influence on the king he served, the Hebrew community, the society, region, and country. He was told, "Those who survived the exile and are back in the province are in great trouble and disgrace. The wall of Jerusalem is broken down, and its gates have been burned with fire" (Nehemiah 1:3). When he heard that, he went there with confidence and with

God's presence, to engage in correcting history. He was determined to bring back what was lost—hope and protection. He repaired what was broken and revived what was neglected, restoring dignity by removing the shame of the past generation.

Three Dimensions of Rebuilding

One of the keys in correcting history is to remove the shame and disappointment of the past by going back to the original plan and purpose of God in standard, worship, and holiness. Spiritual shame can be removed and hope for the future can be reestablished through truth, rebuilding the altar of worship, and restoring the temple of God's dwelling in holiness and greater majesty. Zerubbabel, Joshua, Ezra, and Nehemiah worked to correct history by eradicating the curses of sin on a nation. They dealt with the three dimensions of rebuilding: the altar of worship, the temple of His glorious presence, and a wall of protection and standard. Let's examine these three dimensions more closely.

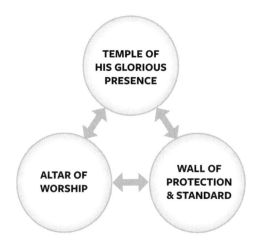

Altar of Worship

First, correcting history requires a personal renewal, which is symbolized by rebuilding the altar. Personal renewal (restoring our hearts to our Creator) must begin with the core issue: worship. The altar of worship is the foundation of a covenant relationship with God, which is why Abraham built altars to God. In the next generation, Isaac also built an altar to the God of his father, Abraham, to confirm the covenant relationship that began with Abraham and continued with his son. Jacob, too, was called to build an altar to receive all that God promised his grandfather and his father.

Every true correction must start with restoration of the altar in our personal lives, to restore our hearts to our Creator. This is the intimate place of worship where our covenant relationship with God is sealed and where our fellowship is fed and sustained by His life-giving presence. Without restoration of the altar, there can be no further meaningful correction of history. The sin of the past, and the guilt and shame of the present, can only be dealt with at the cross of Christ for true freedom. If you desire to know more, consider reading another book Chuck and I co-authored, *Rekindle the Altar Fire* (Chosen, 2020), for a deep revelation of what you should do to overcome your past and come into the powerful presence of God.

Temple of His Glorious Presence

Second, correcting history requires recognizing God's greatness and deeply wanting to abide in His presence. Rebuilding the temple of His glorious presence symbolizes this. The temple is where God's manifested presence, glory, power, majesty, and holiness dwell. God desired a place where He could dwell with His people, so He gave Moses a clear pattern for what the Tabernacle would look like. This Tabernacle was a place of worship. Hosting the presence of God is no small thing and should be considered with fear and trembling. Correcting history means being ready to move everything out of the way to make room for the Lord's manifested presence again, restoring the desire for His presence among His people. "Then Moses said to him, 'If your Presence does not go with us, do not send us up from here'" (Exodus 33:15).

When King Solomon completed the Temple, he dedicated it to the Lord in the assembly of the Israelites. At the end of his dedication, Solomon invited the presence of the Lord into the place prepared for Him. As soon as Solomon finished speaking his prayer, heavenly fire came down and consumed the sacrifices, and the glory of the Lord filled the Temple. In Nehemiah's day, after five godly men led the people into the restored Temple, the Lord promised even greater glory: "'The glory of this present house will be greater than the glory of the former house,' says the LORD Almighty" (Haggai 2:9).

Wall of Protection and Standard

Third, correcting history requires a commitment to protect the glory of God and what He entrusted to us by reestablishing His standard and truth. Nehemiah did this by rebuilding the broken wall. History makers who are committed to correcting history by rebuilding the foundation first start with a personal renewal (rebuilding our personal altar). Second, they understand the greatness of God and are willing to abide in His presence (rebuilding our temple). Third, they protect the Lord's glory and what He has entrusted to us (rebuilding the wall).

In ancient times, cities were walled for protection and defense. The city wall symbolized security and safety. It kept enemies out and citizens safe within. The wall was a high, deep, carefully constructed stone barrier, and the gates set into the wall were the only entry points. During the siege on Jerusalem, the wall had been toppled into heaps of rubble and the gates had been destroyed by fire.

While still in captivity, Nehemiah heard about the Jewish remnant in Jerusalem and the broken wall and gates around the city.

The issue was twofold. First, the gates had been burned down. As a point of entry into a walled city, a gate is a significantly important feature. When the gate is strong and closed, there is no access or fear of invasion. The primary focus of an invading enemy is to destroy the gate. Second, the stone wall around Jerusalem was broken down, causing insecurity for the people, despite the restoration of the altar and Temple. Without a wall, they were defenseless. Restoration can't be completed without building a wall of protection. The wall is needed to protect the altar and Temple of God.

Nehemiah, called by God, found favor with Persian King Artaxerxes and was given permission to return to Jerusalem. The king also guaranteed Nehemiah safe passage for his journey and access to timber from the king's forest. Once Nehemiah surveyed the destruction, he shared his God-inspired vision with the Jewish remnant:

> Then I said to them, "You see the distress that we are in, how Jerusalem lies waste, and its gates are burned with fire. Come and let us build the wall of Jerusalem, that we may no longer be a reproach." And I told them of the hand of my God which had been good upon me, and also of the king's words that he had spoken to me.
>
> So they said, "Let us rise up and build." Then they set their hands to this good work.
>
> Nehemiah 2:17–18 NKJV

The core of restoration is restoring hope. Hope breaks the cycle of destruction by placing faith where fear and doubt once were: "May the God of hope fill you with all joy and peace as you trust in him, so that you may overflow with hope by the power of the Holy Spirit" (Romans 15:13). Hope gives us security about the future, which leads into a life of victory. When things are broken in our personal lives, family, community, or country, it can take away confidence for tomorrow. Restoring a sense of security and protection brings back hope, love, righteousness, unity, and justice, which are needed for a strong and healthy future.

Steps for Rebuilding the Wall

The future doesn't depend on what a person has, but on what his or her hopes and vision are. The starting point is building the wall of protection and the gates to restore confidence. Nehemiah wept when he heard about the broken wall and gates of Jerusalem. God's people felt shame and disgrace because they lacked protection and were unable to defend themselves. In any restoration process, the foundation may be literal, metaphorical, or both. A literal wall is like the restoration of a structure around Jerusalem. Restoring a spiritual wall would be metaphorical. In the spiritual or metaphorical sense, this is the process of restoring broken, neglected spiritual principles, bringing spiritual awakening or revival for the transformation of a society or the Body of Christ. Spiritual renewal brings back God's presence, which is our true protection. In rebuilding the wall of Jerusalem literally and metaphorically, Nehemiah took the following specific steps, which we'll look at one at a time in the rest of this chapter.

Nehemiah discovered the true spiritual condition of Jerusalem. Restoration requires grasping reality, and then bringing about needed change. Nehemiah asked his brother, Hanani, and other men who had come to Jerusalem about the city's condition. He questioned them to get firsthand information. If we don't hear correct information, we can't act correctly. Usually, hearing is what leads to action. "When I heard these things, I sat down and wept. For some days I mourned and fasted and prayed before the God of heaven" (Nehemiah 1:4).

Nehemiah confessed and repented of his sins and the nation's sins. The root cause for lacking protection is spiritual. Why did Nehemiah weep when he heard about Jerusalem's condition? He knew what had caused the destruction of its wall: "I confess the sins we Israelites, including myself and my father's family, have committed against you. We have acted very wickedly toward you. We have not obeyed the commands, decrees and laws you gave your servant Moses" (Nehemiah 1:6–7). Restoring the wall begins by recognizing and acknowledging the broken spiritual condition of individuals, churches, and nations before God.

Nehemiah sought the Lord in fasting and prayer, based on God's covenant with His people. After he prayed, he knew the Lord wanted him to go rebuild the wall. From a strictly human perspective, this would have been unthinkable because of his position in the Babylonian government. Remember, it was the Babylonian government that destroyed the wall of Jerusalem. To ask the same government for permission, time, resources, and protection to go back and rebuild the wall seemed foolish in the natural.

Nehemiah accepted God's calling. He embraced the assignment after much prayer and even though he was afraid of the king's reaction. Repairing broken walls is the core call of everyone committed to God's will. True spirituality involves moving into an extraordinary relationship with God by stepping up to and walking in our high calling. That is what great determination is all about: making a difference and paying the price for the cause of Christ through total obedience.

Nehemiah stood on the promises of God. Though he was far away, Nehemiah's genuine concern was for the city of God. His sadness didn't make him hopeless, however. Rather, his sadness made him turn in hope to the Lord on behalf of his nation. This is a strong character trait of history makers. The basis for his hope was God's promises. After he mourned, fasted, and prayed, he reminded the Lord about the covenant He had made with His people. The covenant was restored through repentance: "But if you return to me and obey my commands, then even if your exiled people are at the farthest horizon, I will gather them from there and bring them to the place I have chosen as a dwelling for my Name" (Nehemiah 1:9). The Lord heard Nehemiah's prayer, and His hand and favor came upon him. This created faith and confidence in Nehemiah as he planned for his journey. The foundation of ever-increasing faith is the Word of God. His presence brings confidence and boldness for our calling, despite opposition and challenges.

Nehemiah asked the Lord for success. Nehemiah asked God for favor with King Artaxerxes: "Give your servant success today by granting him favor in the presence of this man" (Nehemiah 1:11). True spiritual success is the result of God's favor, and His favor is the fruit of His presence. God's presence is what brings desired results, enabling us to rebuild the broken walls in our settings. Nehemiah was a cupbearer to the king. He held a high position, and the king depended on him. He had experience and knowledge, and he was a good manager. Yet he sought the Lord's favor in preparation to rebuild the wall. If we seek the Lord and learn to depend on Him, success is granted, despite the opposition or challenges we might face in the process.

Nehemiah identified himself with the nation. Nehemiah embraced responsibility for the sins of his nation and repented before the Lord, standing in the gap for Israel and Jerusalem. History makers identify themselves with the problem and make themselves available to God. When we accept responsibility instead of blaming others, the Lord uses us to bring a solution. The most effective way of rebuilding broken walls is to stand in the gap. That's what the Lord is seeking. The Lord once told Ezekiel, "I looked for a man among them who would build up the wall and stand before me in the gap on behalf of the land so I would not have to destroy it, but I found none" (Ezekiel 22:30).

Nehemiah prayed for special favor. With His calling, God gives abundant grace. First, God's grace releases favor to do His will, as well as all the provision we need for the vision He gives us. Without the favor of God, no one would be able to serve His purpose.

Second, grace gives us favor in the eyes of other people. These are people we need assistance from, people we will work with, people we lead or serve. The key to accessing God's favor is prayer. Through prayer, we express our total dependency on the Lord, we worship and honor Him, and we acknowledge His ability to do in us and through us what He has promised. We express our faith since it is impossible to please God without faith. Prayer is the key to releasing the great grace and favor we need to fulfill His purpose.

Nehemiah received answers to his prayer to repair the wall of protection. The Lord answered Nehemiah's prayer by giving him special favor in the king's eyes, as well as insight into the time it would take to repair Jerusalem's wall. The Lord's hand also came upon him for protection, guidance, provision, power, and ability. Nehemiah testified to this: "And because the gracious hand of my God was upon me, the king granted my requests" (Nehemiah 2:8). The foundation for restoration is prayer that brings God's presence and His hand to make the impossible possible and the unthinkable a reality. That's why restoration that isn't grounded on prayer is built upon sand, not upon the solid rock of God's promises.

Nehemiah calculated the cost. In addition to his willingness to obey the Lord's will and seek Him in prayer, Nehemiah planned the process of repairing the wall. First, he made a commitment to go back and rebuild. When the king asked him, he prayed again, and then he told the king, "If it pleases the king and if your servant has found favor in his sight, let him send me to the city in Judah where my fathers are buried so that I can rebuild it" (Nehemiah 2:5). Nehemiah wasn't just asking for time off, but also for the king *to send him.* That means this would be considered one of the king's assignments, and the king would take responsibility for provision and protection. What amazing faith and wisdom Nehemiah had! Second, Nehemiah was able to figure out how long the rebuilding would take: "It pleased the king to send me; so I set a time" (Nehemiah 2:6).

Nehemiah had vision and strategy. A king can give provision and provide protection, but vision, strategy, and the blueprint for restoration come only from the Lord. Yes, Nehemiah had a burning passion to restore the wall, but he also had clear vision with a practical, sound strategy to rebuild. Having a burden for the house of God is the starting point, but without clear vision and sound strategy, we cannot bring about the desired restoration. Having a solid, sound strategy, vision, passion, management skills, preparation, and an evaluation procedure in place are part of an effective restoration blueprint. That is why we need all the fivefold ministries to work together in our day, so that they bring about a true rebuilding of the walls protecting the things of the Lord.

Nehemiah assessed and acted. After Nehemiah arrived in Jerusalem, he spent three days assessing the situation without taking any action. After three days, he went around the city at night to see for himself what the Lord had placed upon his heart and to examine the ruins. "By night I went out through the Valley Gate toward the Jackal Wall and the Dung Gate, examining the walls of Jerusalem, which had been broken down, and its gates, which had been destroyed by fire" (Nehemiah 2:13).

Nehemiah completed the work of repairing the wall in 52 days, because of the gracious hand of the Lord upon his life. All of the external and internal challenges were unable to stop him. After Nehemiah heard about the condition of Jerusalem, he fasted and prayed for clearer direction and the right timing. When he felt the time was right, he went to Jerusalem and shared with the people the city's condition, inviting them to rebuild the wall. The Lord confirmed the timing by moving on the king's heart, as well as the people's hearts. Furthermore, Nehemiah built the people's faith by telling them about God's gracious hand upon his life as a leader. He also told them what the king had said and done because of God's hand. This gave them success.

Effective Steps and Strategies

It is crucial in the process of making and correcting history to start with the vital and highly effective steps of having the right motivation, being in prayer, being in the right place, having a clear vision, having a practical and workable strategy, being in the right timing, and having a sign of God's presence.

The most effective strategies for dealing with opposition are understanding the enemy's strategies, knowing the power of God, and clearly identifying what we are called to restore, build, and shape. We cannot build without first restoring, and we cannot shape the future without building a strong, lasting foundation.

We must identify what is broken in our spheres of influence and make a commitment to restore and build on a solid foundation to shape the future.

QUESTIONS FOR ABIDING DEEPER

- What are the areas (walls) in you that need to be rebuilt? What about the broken walls in your culture?
- Do you find it easy to let go of the past to begin correcting history and rebuilding? If not, ask God for the grace to release all blame, like a true history maker.

14

REVEALING HIS GLORY AND HOSTING HIS PRESENCE

ALEMU BEEFTU

Let us bring the ark of our God back to us, for we did not inquire of it during the reign of Saul.

1 Chronicles 13:3

God is looking for someone who reveals His glory, abides in His presence, and shapes the future. Since creation, the call of God on every generation has been to restore what was lost, establish a standard for holiness, and prepare the future generation to see and taste the Lord's goodness. We are called to shape the future through our actions, plans, visions, dreams, and mindset. Shaping the future isn't only dreaming about tomorrow, but is also correcting the past, as we talked about in the previous chapter. By building on a wrong foundation, we can't secure tomorrow's vision.

King David expressed his heart for the coming generation in his prayer: "Even when I am old and gray, do not forsake me, my God, till I declare your power to the next generation, your mighty acts to all who are to come" (Psalm 71:18). What a prayer and vision for the future! No wonder the Lord used David in an amazing way to correct, build, and shape history.

We start building the future by dealing with the past correctly. Our actions become like a two-edged sword: one side corrects the past, while the other side shapes the future. Correcting the past sometimes means cutting out wrong things and removing them from our memories so we can start with a new energy, vision, and hope, without being pulled back by yesterday's shortcoming or failings.

After Moses' death, Joshua led the people into the Promised Land. Once they entered, the Lord told Joshua to remove the reproach of the past by circumcising them. That circumcision removed the reproach of four hundred years in Egypt, as well as the rebellion of forty years in the desert. "And after the whole nation had been circumcised . . . the Lord said to Joshua, 'Today I have rolled away the reproach of Egypt'" (Joshua 5:8–9). Through the circumcision, the people's covenant relationship with God was renewed, and the idol worship, complaining, unbelief, and slavery mindset they had brought from Egypt were dealt with.

We restore our accurate reflection of the Lord's glory by removing all the hindrances and renewing our covenant relationship with God. John the Baptist prepared the way for Jesus by bringing down, lifting up, and making straight the path for the Lord's glory to return to Israel. Preparing the way to reveal His glory means letting go of the past and stretching forward by faith to accept the new things God has for us.

"Forget the former things; do not dwell on the past. See, I am doing a new thing! Now it springs up; do you not perceive it? I am making a way in the wilderness and streams in the wasteland" (Isaiah 43:18–19). We first start with the command "Forget," which includes failing to remember, not recalling, overlooking, disregarding, neglecting, unlearning, and so forth. The second command is that we don't dwell on the past, don't live in it. We are to come out from there and see what's coming. What's coming isn't what we experienced, but is a new thing. Until we perceive the new thing, it's hard to let go of the past. We receive with an open heart what we perceive by faith.

Paul said, "But one thing I do: Forgetting what is behind and straining toward what is ahead" (Philippians 3:13). If we don't let go of the past, we will end up compromising on our goal for the future. Letting go of the past doesn't mean denying past failures. Denying past failures isn't true freedom; it makes us prisoners of yesterday and takes away the joy of hoping for tomorrow. We start reflecting God's glory when we've dealt with the past in the right way. Dealing with the past positions us to prepare the way for His glory to be revealed.

In Isaiah 39, the prophet foretold the Babylonian invasion of Judah and the destruction of the Temple and Jerusalem as a sign of God's judgment. In chapter 40, Isaiah prophesied about restoration that takes place through repentance. Repentance prepares the way for the glory returning to Israel, which is ultimately fulfilled by the coming of the King of glory, Jesus Christ. These are central issues in restoring His glorious presence:

- *Repentance by having a renewed mindset to bear the fruit of righteousness*—"Produce fruit in keeping with repentance" (Luke 3:8).
- *Dealing with personal pride*—"And do not begin to say to yourselves, 'We have Abraham as our father'" (Luke 3:8).
- *Preparing the way for the Lord by making things right, adjusting the value system* (raising the valley, lowering mountains, leveling the path, etc.), and *differentiating between what's eternal and what's temporary* (Isaiah 40:3–5).

- *Making the path straight*—"A voice of one calling in the wilderness, 'Prepare the way for the Lord, make straight paths for him'" (Matthew 3:3).

- *Restoring broken relationships*—"To turn the hearts of the fathers to their children and the disobedient to the wisdom of the righteous—to make ready a people prepared for the Lord" (Luke 1:17 NIV1984).

- *Turning to God*—"He will turn many of the people of Israel to the Lord their God" (Luke 1:16 NET).

- *Welcoming the King of glory*—"But after me comes one who is more powerful than I, whose sandals I am not worthy to carry" (Matthew 3:11).

- *Rekindling the fire of the Holy Spirit*—"He will baptize you with the Holy Spirit and fire" (Matthew 3:11).

Again, I recommend reading our book *Rekindle the Altar Fire* (Chosen, 2020) for a deep revelation of what you should do to overcome your past and come into the powerful presence of God.

Welcoming the King of Glory

"The glory of the Lord shone around them, and they were terrified" (Luke 2:9). This is the same glory Isaiah prophesied: "And the glory of the LORD will be revealed, and all people will see it together. For the mouth of the LORD has spoken" (Isaiah 40:5). This fulfilled prophesy resulted in the full revelation of the glory of God through the birth of Jesus. When the Word became flesh and dwelt among us, He revealed the Father's glory that Isaiah desired: "Oh, that you would rend the heavens and come down, that the mountains would tremble before you!" (Isaiah 64:1).

The greatest thing for God's people is having a true sign of His presence. That was why Moses prayed earnestly for God's presence to go with them; journeying without the manifested presence of God was not worth it. The identity of God's people is His presence, which distinguishes them from all others. "Then Moses said to him, 'If your Presence does not go with us, do not send us up from here'" (Exodus 33:15). When the Lord guaranteed His presence was there, Moses went one step further and asked God to show His glory. In human context, God's presence is the manifestation of His glory. So God declared His glorious name and passed His goodness before Moses by hiding him in the cleft of a rock under His mighty hand (see Exodus 33:21–23). Moses' face was transformed and glowing when he came back to his people because of the Lord's glory.

Welcoming the King of glory requires us to prepare the way and the place for Him. King David started by seeking and bringing back the Ark of His presence. After David became king, he declared the need to bring back God's presence to the nation: "And let us bring again the ark of our God to us, for we did not seek it during the days of Saul" (1 Chronicles 13:3 AMPC).

King Saul was content being king over Israel. For David, however, sitting on the throne without God's presence was unthinkable. He started shepherding God's people by correcting what had gone wrong during the rulership of King Saul. David clearly understood that it's impossible to shepherd God's people without the presence of the Good Shepherd. David declared in worship that the role of the Lord is in the life of His people: "The LORD is my shepherd; I shall not want. He makes me to lie down in green pastures" (Psalm 23:1 NKJV). No wonder the Lord promised His people to give them David as a shepherd. The difference between King Saul and King David is that Saul led and managed, but David shepherded God's people like Jesus, the Good Shepherd, who gave His life for His sheep.

When David returned the Ark, he corrected what had gone wrong during Saul's forty-year reign. Restoring God's glorious presence means bringing back what was neglected, looking for what was missing, searching for the original, going back to the first love, honor, worship, and obedience. The most important point in revealing and reflecting God's glory is restoring what's missing in our relationship with Him. We secure His presence by fulfilling His desire to be amongst His people. His name is Emmanuel—God is with us! There is no greater calling than protecting His presence by being sensitive to His voice and seeking first His Kingdom.

In bringing back the Ark of God's presence and might, David declared that all authority, power, protection, guidance, and worship belonged to the God of Abraham, Isaac, and Jacob. In correcting the history of neglecting God's presence, however, David and the nation sinned by bringing back the Ark on a cart, as we saw in chapter 6. That was contrary to the blueprint in the Word of God. The Ark was to be carried by priests. This resulted in God's judgment: "The LORD's anger burned against Uzzah, and he struck him down because he had put his hand on the ark. So he died there before God" (1 Chronicles 13:10). Sincerity and commitment are not enough to host His presence; you need total obedience to His Word.

David and the people also didn't prepare a place for the Lord's Ark the first time. What we do and how we do it matters to God. But David learned from his mistakes and corrected them. As the nation's leader, he admitted this mistake publicly: "We did not inquire of him about how to do it in the prescribed way" (1 Chronicles 15:13). This time, David prepared a place for the Ark of the Covenant before they brought it back: "He prepared a place for the ark of God and pitched a tent for it" (verse 1). This time, the priests followed Moses' instruction and carried the Ark in the prescribed way. As they brought it back, David himself put on a priestly garment, rather than his kingly clothes, to worship the Lord. "Now David was clothed in a robe of fine linen, as were all the Levites who were carrying the ark" (verse 27).

David's sincere repentance greatly pleased the Lord. Before my daughter and son took water baptism, I took the time to teach them about salvation and the meaning of water baptism. A week before the baptismal day, I asked both to choose one character from the Bible to share, or a passage they could share, prior to the baptism celebration. My daughter chose Esther because of this queen's determination to save her generation. My son's choice was David. His reason was simple, yet profound: "David did not have any problem in repenting and making things right with God whenever he messed up."

On that journey of restoring the Ark for the second time, God gave David one of my favorite passages, 1 Chronicles 16. In fact, the name of our ministry, Gospel of Glory, has its name and mission based on 1 Chronicles 16:24: "Declare his glory among the nations, his marvelous deeds among all peoples." Since its inception, Gospel of Glory's motto has been "Declare His glory among the nations!"

The Restoration of David's Tent

The Lord honored the return of the Ark and the tent David had built for it. As a result of David's efforts to correct things, God promised to restore the tent of His presence for the future generation: "In that day I will restore David's fallen tent. I will repair its broken places, restore its ruins, and build it as it used to be" (Amos 9:11 NIV1984). It isn't only the promise of repairing and installing it for future generations; it's also the place for seeking God's presence. The apostles declared the fulfillment of this at the inception of the early Church: "'That the rest of mankind may seek the Lord, even all the Gentiles who bear my name, says the Lord, who does these things'—things known from long ago" (Acts 15:17–18).

The restoration of David's tent also signifies the restoration of a sincere, personal relationship, and worship without ritual exercises. David was a prophet who understood the holiness of God and led his people with prophetic insight and wisdom. His worship songs in Psalms 22, 23, 24, and others prophesied about the Lord Jesus. David was also a king and warrior who prepared and raised mighty men in his kingdom. David's kingdom was a picture of Jesus Christ's Kingdom.

In the last days, the core of the restoration of David's tent is to bring about the fullness of what God showed us through David's life in the Old Testament—that we are to:

- Enter into God's presence with worship and praise.
- Understand the majesty and holiness of God.
- Walk and minister with true spiritual revelation.
- Serve God's purpose with ever-increasing anointing.
- Open the gates for the King of glory, for every tongue and every tribe to bring Him sacrifices and praises.
- Exercise spiritual authority to advance the Kingdom of God.
- Raise a mighty army for Kingdom life and work.
- Balance priestly worship with kingly authority.
- Shepherd the saints with God's compassion.
- Demonstrate the power of the Gospel and declare God's holiness and glory so that the nations will cry out, "Holy, holy, holy is the LORD Almighty; the whole earth is full of his glory" (Isaiah 6:3).

The two wings of David's tent were worship and prophetic revelation. These were based on a kingly anointing and authority. As in David's day, today the Lord wants to restore priestly worship, prophetic revelation, and kingly authority to advance His Kingdom. David's tent in the Old Testament functioned without specific regulations (whereas the Temple would have many). Since it was a tent, it was open to everyone who desired to worship the Lord in spirit and truth. The tent was for everybody!

In my opinion, there is no history maker like David. He restored God's glory and prepared the next generation for the future. He started making history before he sat on the throne of Israel. As a young man, he was sent by his father to take supplies to his brothers at the front lines. He returned carrying Goliath's head and sword! A young boy killing a giant warrior with a small stone? Yes! David made history. He went in the name of the Lord, with faith. He freed God's people from the fear of the enemy and honored God's name. David showed that the name of the God of Abraham, Isaac, and Jacob is more powerful than any human power.

David also established a standard of excellence by making history in everything he did for the rest of his life: "And he became more and more powerful, because the LORD God Almighty was with him" (2 Samuel 5:10). Because of God's presence with him, and because he depended on and sought God, he became stronger and stronger. He became the standard for every king who came after him.

David also shaped the future by focusing on God's presence and living as a man after God's own heart. He reestablished God's glorious presence by bringing back the Ark of God and preparing a place for it. He abided in the presence of God through personal worship and through organizing the priests according to their gifts, to worship the Lord continually.

QUESTIONS FOR ABIDING DEEPER

- Where in your life do you see a need for repentance? In what ways can you prepare a place for God's presence by correcting history in that area?
- From the list earlier in this chapter, which of the central issues for restoring God's glorious presence are you in the midst of right now?

15

DECLARE HIS POWER AND SHAPE THE FUTURE

ALEMU BEEFTU

Declare his glory among the nations, his marvelous deeds among all peoples.

1 Chronicles 16:24

Making history and correcting the past lead us into an extraordinary relationship with God. Our God is the same yesterday, today, and forever. The past and the future are the same in His presence, so making history can't be separated from shaping the future.

David understood this truth and wasn't satisfied just correcting the past, returning the Ark of God's presence, and building the tent for it. He desired to build a temple for the Lord. David's priorities were different. Whether he was a shepherd or a king, in the field or in the palace, it was all about his God. David knew and fully accepted the anointing to be a son. The Lord said of him, "I have found David my servant; with my sacred oil I have anointed him. . . . And I will appoint him to be my firstborn, the most exalted of the kings of the earth" (Psalm 89:20, 27). God called him "my firstborn," and David responded by calling God "my Father." From then on, David's relationship with God was top priority.

"I have installed my king on Zion, my holy mountain," the Lord said (Psalm 2:6). That's the reason why David was unable to settle without God's presence. For David, the temple he wanted to build was meant to proclaim the holiness and majesty of God the Creator, King, Savior, sustainer, restorer, and provider. However, the Lord told him that he wasn't the one who would build it. Instead, it would be his son Solomon. Yet God was pleased with David's yearning to build a temple in addition to the tent, which reflected characteristics in David that the Lord would like to see in every generation. These characteristics include:

- *Worship*—God wants to restore the tent of worship in Spirit and truth. Every generation has been evaluated not on people's activities, but on their worship of God and their obedience to His Word. The basis for future evaluation is also worship. John wrote in Revelation, "I was given a reed like a measuring rod and was told, 'Go and measure the temple of God and the altar, and count the worshipers there'" (Revelation 11:1 NIV1984).

- *Walking with God*—David's life was about walking with God, about his relationship with the Lord. God continues to restore personal relationships such as David had as a son with God as Father. This isn't about tradition or culture, but about approaching God's throne of grace! Walking with God started in the Garden and became the standard throughout the Old Testament. The Lord wants to restore our walk with Him into its fullness. That kind of walk transforms us into His likeness. "Whoever claims to live in him must walk as Jesus did" (1 John 2:6 NIV1984).

- *Working with God*—David not only walked with God, but also worked with God. Samuel summarized David's life like this: "In everything he did he had great success, because the LORD was with him" (1 Samuel 18:14).

- *Walking in prophetic revelation*—David saw what was coming and focused on what ought to be. He saw the greatness, majesty, protection, provision, power, mercy, and holiness of God: "LORD, our Lord, how majestic is your name in all the earth! You have set your glory in the heavens" (Psalm 8:1).

- *Warring for generational freedom*—David's war was not for himself. He focused on the purpose of God and the generations that would follow. He started warring for the glory of God and the freedom of his people before he sat on the throne as king of Israel. God wanted to restore that fervor for the glory of His name and the freedom of His people.

- *A willingness to correct the past*—David brought back the Ark of God's presence, which had been neglected for many years, by mobilizing his people.

- *A spirit of repentance*—David lived his life with a spirit of humility and repentance: "My sacrifice, O God, is a broken spirit; a broken and contrite heart you, God, will not despise" (Psalm 51:17).

- *Increased anointing*—David was anointed three times. Because of this, he established a sonship relationship with God, and he became a radical worshiper and king of Israel. The intensity of the anointing increased with his authority and responsibility. One aspect of the restoration of David's tent is the ever-increasing anointing to move from glory to glory.

- *Dynasty*—God promised David that his throne would last forever. Part of the restoration of David's tent was kingly authority and a priestly role. Dynasty is about blood relationship. The Word became flesh to establish that kind of blood relationship between Jesus and us. Now, He has made us kings and priests in His Kingdom, but He is King of kings and Lord of lords forevermore.

- *Being a shepherd*—David was known for being a shepherd for God's people. The Lord raised him to protect, guide, and lead them: "I will raise up over them one Shepherd and He shall feed them, even My Servant David; He shall feed them and He shall be their Shepherd" (Ezekiel 34:23 AMPC).

- *Order*—David brought order into everything during both King Saul's reign and later in his own kingdom. He organized warriors, worshipers, scribes, musicians, singers, prophets, and so forth. The people said of David, "In times past, even when Saul was king, it was you who led out and brought in Israel; and the LORD your God said to you, 'You shall shepherd My people Israel, and you shall be prince and leader over My people Israel'" (1 Chronicles 11:2 AMP). God is in the process of restoring divine order—the full manifestation of His glory—in His Kingdom.

- *Holiness*—More than any king in the history of Israel, David understood God's holiness. David's life was guided by the fear, wisdom, covenant, mercy, praises, worship, honor, adoration, and holiness of God.

Putting the Pattern in Place

When David heard from Nathan the prophet what the Lord had said about building the Temple, he was overwhelmed with the goodness and mercy of the Lord. He responded to the message by sitting before God in a spirit of worship, praise, and thankfulness for what the Lord had revealed. Before his death, he started making extensive preparations to help young Solomon build God's Temple. He told Solomon, "You have many workers: stonecutters, masons and carpenters, as well as those skilled in every kind of work in gold and silver, bronze and iron—craftsmen beyond number. Now begin the work, and the LORD be with you" (1 Chronicles 22:15–16).

The process that brought David to where he received the Temple pattern is significant. First David desired to build the Temple so the nation would honor the holiness of God and embrace a holy reverence for Him. David oversaw all the preparatory planning for the building, flowing from a pure heart and a desire to honor God. The apostle Paul later expressed the same motives to Timothy for building God's Kingdom: "The goal of this command is love, which comes from a pure heart and a good conscience and a sincere faith" (1 Timothy 1:5).

In addition, David went to the Lord to ask for a pattern for the building. The Lord wrote with His hand the details of the pattern and gave it to David (see 1 Chronicles 28:19). The Spirit of God also gave him an understanding of the necessary details, along with specifications of every aspect of the Temple. David sought the Lord for a revelation and waited upon the Lord to receive the blueprint, for the sake of the next generation.

With a pure heart and right motive that started in David and continued in Solomon, the Temple was built to last and to display God's holiness. God shows us the pattern for our time, too, according to our heart's desire. The passion of our heart is the driving engine of our lives. David sought the Lord for the pattern so his son could build according to God's plan. Many times, we see a pattern and can go as far as identifying both the human and financial resources to build it. However, we don't have the patience to wait upon the Lord for revelation about the pattern. We pass on a formula that has no spirit or life to it. Without revelation, the pattern becomes a lifeless system without any fruit. Today, we need leaders with the spirit and determination of David—those who are willing to ask for a life-giving pattern for the next generation.

David also provided building materials like gold, silver, bronze, cedar logs, and iron to make nails. He ordered the people to help Solomon build the Temple and appointed a supervisor for the work: "Of these, twenty-four thousand are to be in charge of the work of the temple of the LORD and six thousand are to be officials and judges. Four thousand are to be gatekeepers and four thousand are to praise the LORD with the musical instruments I have provided for that purpose" (1 Chronicles 23:4–5).

David set apart the priests to consecrate the most holy things, offer sacrifices before the Lord, minister before Him, and pronounce blessings in the name of the Lord forever: "The sons of Amram: Aaron and Moses. Aaron was set apart, he and his descendants forever, to consecrate the most holy things, to offer sacrifices before the LORD, to minister before him and to pronounce blessings in his name forever" (1 Chronicles 23:13).

David set apart prophets to prophesy with musical instruments, and singers (see 1 Chronicles 25). He put gatekeepers in their places (see 1 Chronicles 26). He charged his son Solomon to build the house of the Lord:

> Now, my son, the LORD be with you, and may you have success and build the house of the LORD your God, as he said you would. May the LORD give you discretion and understanding when he puts you in command over Israel, so that you may keep the law of the LORD your God.
>
> 1 Chronicles 22:11–12

For David, the most important preparation was preparing his son Solomon for the purpose of God. He did this before he gave Solomon the pattern to start building. Without divine wisdom, just having a pattern wasn't enough to build the Temple for God's glory.

Passing on Divine Wisdom to Live By

David gave Solomon the following wisdom not only as his earthly father, but also as an anointed child and prophet of God who walked with God all his life. The divine wisdom he passed on to young Solomon came out of a lifetime walk with God and included experiencing God's presence, having a heart after God, loving God, loving the Word of God, and acknowledging God's glory and holiness. So along with a divine pattern for the Temple, David gave Solomon divine wisdom to live by that we would also do well to live by:

- *Know your God.* Gain knowledge of your Father. The psalms David wrote show that the desire of his heart was to dwell in God's presence and know Him intimately.
- *Worship Him.* Worship, adore, and obey Him. What we do for God should reflect a life of obedience.
- *Serve Him wholeheartedly.* Servanthood requires having an excellent spirit. Joshua and Caleb obeyed God wholeheartedly because they had a different spirit from the rest of the community, who rebelled against God.
- *Have a willing mind to do His will.* A willing mind is renewed by the Holy Spirit and the Word of God. A renewed mind can produce an acceptable sacrifice.
- *Seek Him with all your heart and soul.* Seeking God creates a desire in us to be in His presence. "Now devote your heart and soul to seeking the LORD your God. Begin to build the sanctuary of the LORD God, so that you may bring the ark of the covenant of the LORD and the sacred articles belonging to God into the temple that will be built for the Name of the LORD" (1 Chronicles 22:19).
- *Have right motives.* Serving God is about attitude more than activities. Attitude is the expression of our inner motives.

- *Don't forsake Him.* Don't compromise on the statutes of the Lord.
- *Know your calling!* God calls us to Himself to qualify us for His purpose.
- *Be strong.* "Be strengthened in the Lord" (Ephesians 6:10 NET).
- *Do the work.* Be committed and stay faithful.
- *Encourage yourself in the Lord.* The greatest weapon of the enemy is discouragement.
- *Don't be afraid.* Fear creates doubt and destroys faith.
- *Dwell in His presence.* Moses' prayer was for God's presence. When His presence is with us, we have everything since He is the "Great I Am"!
- *Know He will finish the work.* God starts with us what He is already finishing.
- *Believe you are not alone.* When God sends us, He goes with us. Others who love Him will join us.
- *Know provision is ready.* God provides for what He initiates.
- *Know you are given authority.* Anointing is delegated authority.

King Solomon built the Temple according to the pattern passed to him by his father, and with the wisdom of God and His provision. The Ark and other holy items were brought from the tent into the Temple to complete the process. The tent was a temporary dwelling, while the Temple was a permanent dwelling. The Temple was like the Tabernacle in its setup; it was also built according to the pattern and received God's approval through fire and His glory:

When Solomon finished praying, fire came down from heaven and consumed the burnt offering and the sacrifices, and the glory of the

LORD filled the temple. The priests could not enter the temple of the LORD because the glory of the LORD filled it.

2 Chronicles 7:1–2

What an awesome sight! The Temple was built according to the pattern and was accepted. The prayer was heard, and fire came down to establish God's presence. By sending the fire and filling the place with His glory, God established a standard for His Temple. There, the Lord displayed His holiness for His people to fear and honor Him. There was one other time previously when the Israelites had seen the glory of the Lord on a mountain, like a fire. This was the second time the Lord had sent His fire and glory at the same time.

Establishing God's Lasting Presence

The Temple was built for the Lord to dwell in not only among the tribes, but also in the land so that those who were near and far, in both present and future generations, the nation of Israel and the Gentiles, would all see His holiness: "This is the place of my throne and the place for the soles of my feet. This is where I will live among the Israelites forever" (Ezekiel 43:7).

Receiving the pattern, understanding it, being faithful to follow it, and passing it to the next generation to build are a must. The Temple was built to show the presence of God and to draw people to come to His house: "In the last days the mountain of the Lord's temple will be established as the highest of the mountains; it will be exalted above the hills, and all nations will stream to it" (Isaiah 2:2).

God gave the Temple pattern to David to establish His lasting presence in Israel and Jerusalem. The purpose was to bring change and transformation not only to the faithful worshipers, but also to the city, the nation, and all nations since His house is to be called the house of prayer. Once the Temple was built according to the pattern, His glory and fire came down. "The name of the city from that time on will be: THE LORD IS THERE" (Ezekiel 48:35).

The Temple was meant to reestablish the holiness of God in tangible ways to individuals, families, communities, cities, and nations, so others could magnify, exalt, and glorify His holy name. Confirmed through Ezekiel's vision of the Temple over and over again, both the building and restoration of the Temple established a permanent presence of God in the land and among His people. The Temple declared the holiness of God, released the fullness of His glory, brought the holy fear and reverence of God, and established divine order. The divine pattern reveals divine order so future generations can follow by living in worship, holiness, relationship, commitment to God's purpose, and care for the next generation's success.

QUESTIONS FOR ABIDING DEEPER

- Have you received the right pattern for your calling, so you can show God's holiness and reveal His glory through it? In other words, do you study His Word and have a willing heart to follow the Holy Spirit's lead daily, so you can discern and carry out God's will for your life?

- Do you have the right heart, motive, and commitment to receive the right pattern, so you can pass it on to the next generation? Like David, what characteristics display this in your life?

16

WALKING UNDER AN OPEN HEAVEN

Alemu Beeftu

But Stephen, full of the Holy Spirit, looked up to heaven and saw the glory of God, and Jesus standing at the right hand of God. "Look," he said, "I see heaven open and the Son of Man standing at the right hand of God."

Acts 7:55–56

Walking under an open heaven refers to our ongoing relationship with the Lord. In the early chapters of this book, we discussed Enoch walking with and being taken by God. He started his walk with God under an open heaven and finished life without returning to what he had left behind when he started his walk with God. That's moving from glory to glory in spiritual life and our relationship with the Lord.

Jesus came to open the heavens in order for God's glory to come to earth. His birth opened the heavens and gave us access to the Father. He became the only entry point to having an eternal relationship with God and staying in His presence, even when we are on earth. He referred to Himself as the only true door that no one can shut, for those who would like to come to the Father through Him.

The concept of an open heaven refers to a desire for God's presence among His people to protect, guide, provide, and create genuine, tangible signs of His presence through His acts of mercy and grace. A closed heaven refers to God's judgment, while an open heaven signifies His mercy and compassion. The first family, Adam and Eve, started under an open heaven with God. However, because of sin, they were not only put out of the Garden of Eden, but were also removed from fellowship with Him. Closing the Garden was also a picture of the broken relationship resulting in curses rather than blessings: "Cursed is the ground because of you; through painful toil you will eat food from it all the days of your life" (Genesis 3:17).

Since that time, the desire of every sincere follower of God is to have the same kind of fellowship with God that Adam and Eve began with, under an open heaven. This same desire was also the prayer of the prophets. As Isaiah cried out, "Oh, that you would rend the heavens and come down, that the mountains would tremble before you!" (Isaiah 64:1).

Ezekiel started his ministry under an open heaven, where he experienced the touch of God: "The heavens were opened and I saw visions of God" (Ezekiel 1:1). "There the hand of the LORD was on him" (verse 3). That leads into true worship. True worship is the key to walking under an open heaven. By neglecting the altar of God, the Israelites brought a curse upon themselves. The Old Testament prophets were called and anointed by God to bring correction through repentance, in order to bring back an open heaven's blessings. The prophets started their ministry under an open heaven by receiving a clear vision from God. Here are some examples (note that some of the minor prophets also had very similar experiences to these):

> *Abraham*—His unique relationship with God, under an open heaven, gave Abram the opportunity to become a friend of God with his new identity. "But you, Israel, my servant, Jacob, whom I have chosen, you descendants of Abraham my friend" (Isaiah 41:8; see also 2 Chronicles 20:7).
>
> *Moses*—He "saw the God of Israel" (Exodus 24:10).
>
> *Ezekiel*—"The heavens were opened and I saw visions of God" (Ezekiel 1:1). "There before me was the glory of the God of Israel, as in the vision I had seen in the plain" (Ezekiel 8:4).
>
> *Isaiah*—"I saw the Lord, high and exalted, seated on a throne; and the train of His robe filled the temple" (Isaiah 6:1).
>
> *Daniel*—"In my vision at night I looked, and there before me was one like a son of man, coming with the clouds of heaven. He approached the Ancient of Days and was led into his presence" (Daniel 7:13).

Living under an open heaven separated true prophets of God from false prophets. True prophets started in God's presence, heard His voice, were sensitive to it, and walked with Him daily. An open heaven is a sign of God's manifested presence. However, the nation of Israel didn't respond in a true spirit of repentance for a long time, or dwell under an open heaven. For four hundred years there were closed heavens because of this, without the voice and vision of God, until the Lord sent John the Baptist. After rebuking the priests for their sin, a promise was given to open the heavens again.

Jesus and an Open Heaven

An open heaven symbolizes the manifest presence of God in the context of our relationship with Him. It is about knowing Him, establishing our personal identity, and affirming our prophetic destiny so we can fulfill our divine purpose on earth. The concept of an open heaven can't be a reality without understanding and walking in a covenant relationship. When the glory of God was going to be revealed for all humanity on earth, John the Baptist came with the anointing of Elijah to preach repentance. He preached with a prophetic voice to prepare the way, coming out of the wilderness to announce the arrival of Jesus. John came to give direction with the spirit of a true prophet.

Elijah had a message that closed and opened the heavens. Israel's sins included rejecting God's covenant, breaking down His altars, and putting His prophets to death with the sword. Elijah prayed for the Lord to close the heavens and stop the rain that signified God's blessings. For three and half years, there was then no rain in the land. After that, Elijah restored the altar, turning the people's hearts back to God. He brought the voice of the prophet to life again by asking God for fire and then rain. John the Baptist was sent in the spirit and power of Elijah. He prepared the way for the Messiah to open the heavens that had been closed for four hundred years. To do this, Jesus went to the Jordan at the beginning of His ministry and was baptized by John:

> As soon as Jesus was baptized, he went up out of the water. At that moment heaven was opened, and he saw the Spirit of God descending like a dove and alighting on him. And a voice from heaven said, "This is my Son, whom I love; with him I am well pleased."
>
> Matthew 3:16–17

The first thing that happened in Jesus' ministry was that heaven was opened, meaning the curse was broken and relationship was restored between God and His people. An open heaven is both a sign and an invitation from the Lord for a new beginning, with a new level of relationship, revelation, restoration, and recovery. Other signs included a connection between heaven and earth, with God releasing ministering angels, prophetic visions for the future, and a manifestation of His glory (see Revelation 4:1; Acts 7).

An open heaven is all about relationship with our Creator, Redeemer, King, and counselor. God's invitation from the beginning has been *Come, turn, and return to Me*. The core message of the Bible is *Come*:

- *Come to the water* (Isaiah's message).
- *Come and live* (Ezekiel's message).
- *Come and follow Me* (Jesus' invitation).
- *Come and see* (Jesus' invitation).
- *Come and rest* (Jesus' invitation).
- *Come and eat* (Jesus' invitation).
- *Come up here* (the Father's invitation).

An open heaven is first established for a relationship with God. This is an invitation to the throne room to see the glory of the King and His Kingdom. When Isaiah entered the throne room, he saw the Lord on His throne. He also saw the King and Kingdom: "The whole earth is full of his glory" (Isaiah 6:3).

Second, revelation opens when we are under an open heaven. In relationship with the eternal God, we walk in true revelation that the Holy Spirit gives us continually. The invitation is "Come up here, and I will show you what must take place after this" (Revelation 4:1). When we are under an open heaven, we see clearly both what is here now and what is yet to come.

Third, an open heaven is about restoration. Under an open heaven, the Lord restores to us what the enemy has stolen in the past. "See if I will not throw open the floodgates of heaven and pour out so much blessing that you will not have room enough for it" (Malachi 3:10 NIV1984). When we are in right relationship with

God, we walk in the revelation of His Kingdom. It's natural for a believer to seek right standing with Him, which releases Kingdom blessings and restores what was lost in the past season.

Ministering under an Open Heaven

No wonder Jesus started His ministry under an open heaven. When Jesus came out of the water and prayed, the following things took place immediately: the Holy Spirit rested upon Him, He was filled with the Holy Spirit, and He was led by the Spirit to defeat Satan in the wilderness. First, Jesus was empowered by the Holy Spirit for the call on His life and was anointed by the Spirit to fulfill His prophetic destiny:

> Jesus returned to Galilee in the power of the Spirit, and news about Him spread through the whole countryside. He was teaching in their synagogues, and everyone praised him. He went to Nazareth, where he had been brought up, and on the Sabbath day he went into the synagogue, as was his custom. He stood up to read, and the scroll of the prophet Isaiah was handed to him.
>
> Luke 4:14–17

Then second, the voice of the Father came. The four hundred years of silence were broken, and the voice of God was heard by those who watched Jesus' baptism. God spoke to the people, saying that Jesus was His Son, whom He loved and was well pleased with. What a confirmation of Jesus' life! It was an awesome way to start His ministry based on relationship and love.

The New Testament pattern of ministry is a life of testimony. Ministry is a by-product of a life of obedience, true love, and sincere worship and praise. Jesus both started and completed His public ministry under an open heaven: "While he was blessing them, he left them and was taken up into heaven. Then they worshiped him and returned to Jerusalem with great joy. And they stayed continually at the temple, praising God" (Luke 24:51–53).

The most important thing about walking under an open heaven is having access to the throne room of God, despite our circumstances, just as Stephen did: "'Look,' he said, 'I see heaven open and the Son of Man standing at the right hand of God'" (Acts 7:56). The testimony of the apostle John is very similar: "After this I looked, and there before me was a door standing open in heaven" (Revelation 4:1). John stayed under an open heaven every day of his earthly ministry. That's the New Testament pattern.

This is part of a balancing act—walking under an open heaven, as well as opening doors and ancient gates for the King of glory to come in and establish His ever-increasing Kingdom power and authority, so that every tongue and every tribe would cry out together,

> You are worthy to take the scroll and to open its seals, because you were slain, and with your blood you purchased for God persons from every tribe and language and people and nation. You have made them to be a kingdom and priests to serve our God, and they will reign on the earth.
>
> Revelation 5:9–10

Open Heaven, Doors, and Gates

Let's look closely at the concepts of an open heaven, open doors, and open gates so we see the full picture. These three concepts are mentioned throughout the Bible. Understanding their relationship is key for our relationship with God, for establishing our prophetic destiny, and for understanding our role in Kingdom work. An open heaven is a divine invitation for a relationship with God, for covenant and intimacy. Open doors are a divine invitation to live a life of obedience and run the race faithfully, for the glory of God. Open gates are an invitation for the Kingdom mandate to honor Him, as we prepare the way for the full manifestation so that the nations will see and honor the King of glory, who is coming soon.

In covenant, God opens heaven over us and opens doors before us so that we as His children can open the gates of our lives, ministries, cities, and nations for the establishment of His Kingdom authority (see Psalm 24:7–10). An open heaven affirms our covenantal relationship with God for a greater, deeper revelation that leads to true, lasting transformation in every dimension of our lives.

When God opens heaven over us for a true and lasting relationship, our fellowship with Him is affirmed. God's blessings are released, and His approval is declared. When He opens doors, our calling is realized, and a true commission to carry out His purpose is affirmed. The bridge between the heavens and earth becomes tangible, and the Lord's Prayer is answered: "Let your will be done on earth as it is in heaven." This gives Kingdom workers the keys of the Kingdom to open the gate for the King to come in, and they receive authority to speak to the ancient gates to open up: "Lift up your heads, you gates; be lifted up, you ancient doors, that the King of glory may come in" (Psalm 24:7). The King comes to reign and rule. This is the context of Revelation 11:15: "The kingdom of the world has become the kingdom of our Lord and of his Messiah, and he will reign for ever and ever."

An open heaven over you is a divine invitation not only for a new relationship, but for a lasting relationship. Open doors represent opportunities God provides for us to walk through in obedience and by faith, to fulfill our calling. Our calling and prophetic destiny are to declare the glory of King Jesus on earth by opening the gates and introducing Him as the King of kings and Lord of lords, and as the Savior of the world.

In summary, this is what it means to restore the revelation of His glory, to abide in His presence daily through true worship, and to declare His glory among the nations until He comes back. As we consider these concepts, let's make a firm decision to do these important things:

- First, let's stay under an open heaven by protecting our relationship with God and responding to heaven's invitation to "Come up here" (Revelation 4:1).
- Second, in a spirit of obedience and sincere faith, let's receive the power of the Holy Spirit and the revelation of God's Word to know and walk through the open doors He places before us every day (see Revelation 3:7–8).
- Third, let's know our biblically based value system, establish our identity, and commit to our purpose of making the King of glory known.

An open heaven signifies our relationship with God. It reflects our true identity in Him and reveals Him to the earth through us. Open doors are opportunities to fulfill our calling to open the gates and welcome the King of glory into our spheres of influence. That is abiding in His presence!

QUESTIONS FOR ABIDING DEEPER

- How can you restore your reflection and revelation of God's glory on the earth daily?
- What are small steps you can take to get into God's presence? What happens inside and out when you abide there continually?

17

STAKE YOUR CLAIM
FROM YOUR ABIDING PLACE

CHUCK D. PIERCE

When we submit our spirit to God's Spirit, we then have a positional place in which we are seated. From this heavenly place, we have access to rule and reign in the earthly realm. We can gain wisdom from heaven into any situation we must face on earth. There is a presence-and-glory war going on, however. The battle is to stay positioned and never allow the conditions and blueprints of the world to conform us to the structures that daily attempt to order and saturate our thoughts (see Romans 12:1–2; 1 Corinthians 2:7–8; Ephesians 1; 2).

Much of this chapter is adapted from "The Presence-and-Glory War: Is Your Lampstand Burning?," chapter 5 in my book *God's Unfolding Battle Plan: A Field Manual for Advancing the Kingdom of God* (Minneapolis: Chosen, 2007), 109–137. I have included it here to help you understand how important it is for us to stake our claim from our abiding place in the presence of God and win territory for the Kingdom. Understanding there's a glory war going on is key to continually abiding in God's presence and reflecting His glory to the earth.

We all have a portion in the earth. That portion is called inheritance. You have a glory in you waiting to be activated that allows you to rule your portion. God's desire is to flood this earth with His glory. Habakkuk 2:14 (NKJV) says, "For the earth will be filled with the knowledge of the glory of the LORD, as the waters cover the sea." The thing that prevents God's glory from doing so is the evil in this world, and this is the essence of the presence-and-glory war.

The enemy can only mimic the truth. This has always been the case. We find plenty of people in the Bible who were able to predict the future, yet they had aligned themselves with the enemy. How much more, then, is the God of all truth willing to reveal His plans for the future to His own children? Prophecy—which is simply the testimony of Jesus' reign in the coming days—is all about vision. And in the presence of God, there is perfect vision. Habakkuk 2:1–4 (NKJV) says,

> I will stand my watch and set myself on the rampart, and watch to see what He will say to me, and what I will answer when I am corrected. Then the LORD answered me and said: "Write the vision and make it plain on tablets, that he may run who reads it. For the vision is yet for an appointed time; but at the end it will speak, and it will not lie. Though it tarries, wait for it; because it will surely come, it will not tarry. Behold the proud, his soul is not upright in him; but the just shall live by his faith."

When we live in the Spirit in our abiding place and see by the Spirit, we gain vision for our future. Not only does God reorder our time, but He also positions us in a place so that He can extend the horizon line of heaven and cause us to "see" what He sees. This is what makes us a prophetic people. Acts 17:24–27 (NKJV) says,

> God, who made the world and everything in it, since He is Lord of heaven and earth, does not dwell in temples made with hands. Nor

is He worshiped with men's hands, as though He needed anything, since He gives to all life, breath, and all things. And He has made from one blood every nation of men to dwell on all the face of the earth, and has determined their preappointed times and the boundaries of their dwellings, so that they should seek the Lord, in the hope that they might grope for Him and find Him, though He is not far from each one of us.

When we are at the right place at the right time, the Lord "pro-horizons" us, or extends our horizon line so that we can see farther than ever before. We are not a people limited to the finite space that we are in. We are a people filled with vision. We can *sense* His presence, *feel* His presence, *see* His presence, and *move in* His presence.

As I mentioned before, God has promised to cover the earth with His glory (see Habakkuk 2:14). I believe this was His original intent when He planted the Garden and gave it to the human race. He wanted us to cultivate that garden and live in communion with Him so that He could give us a vision of how to effectively invade the whole earth with His presence. However, when we listened to the enemy, our perfect communion was broken with God and our vision became hindered.

The same principle applies today. If we adhere to the plans of Satan rather than listening to God's voice, we limit God's presence from moving through us and increasing our boundaries. Because of this, there is a huge war raging over His presence. The enemy does all he can to prevent us from seeing what the Lord wants us to see. Satan longs for us not to have vision for our future. Remember, without a vision, we perish (see Proverbs 29:18).

You have a Garden! It is your sphere of authority, with boundaries that you are meant to keep. You must watch after, cultivate, and protect your Garden so it can be filled with God's presence. This will necessitate some battles because the presence-and-glory war is a fierce one—which is why it's so vitally important for us to stake our claim from our abiding place in God's presence. But as always, God has a plan for the ultimate victory.

There is a fierce war that wages over occupying the atmosphere of this earth. Neighborhoods, cities, regions, nations, continents—each has atmospheric boundaries that have either been declared for the purposes of darkness or for housing God's glory. If we read Habakkuk 2:14 with this understanding, we see that the Lord already has a plan to remove evil that is blocking His presence and glory from invading the entire earth realm. His Word declares that "the earth *will be* filled" (emphasis added), which means that the plan of fullness He has for the earth *must be* manifested.

You have had a future—an expected end of success, from the day you were knit together in your mother's womb. In the midst of our conflicts, we must never forget that God has a plan for our lives. Many times darkness wants to rule through fear to stop us from entering into the ultimate plan the Lord has for us. We must never forget that His plan is good. We must also never forget that darkness cannot dwell in our abiding place.

In the book of Jeremiah, God asked the prophet to stake his claim on the future by buying a field that was about to go into desolation. Amid all the darkness surrounding Jerusalem at the time, Jeremiah prophesied that God would eventually restore Israel and Judah, and a remnant would be saved. You must prophesy your future. You must decree heaven's will into the earth's atmosphere. This is how Yeshua taught His disciples to pray (see Luke 11).

We are not perfect, but we have perfection built into our spiritual DNA. When we negate our position of abiding and stray from the Lord, He offers a way to bring us back and restore His plan for us. He has a future of prosperity for us. Jeremiah 31:23–33 (NKJV) says,

> Thus says the LORD of hosts, the God of Israel: "They shall again use this speech in the land of Judah and in its cities, when I bring back their captivity: 'The LORD bless you, O home of justice, and

mountain of holiness!' And there shall dwell in Judah itself, and in all its cities together, farmers and those going out with flocks. For I have satiated the weary soul, and I have replenished every sorrowful soul."

After this I awoke and looked around, and my sleep was sweet to me.

"Behold, the days are coming, says the LORD, that I will sow the house of Israel and the house of Judah with the seed of man and the seed of beast. And it shall come to pass, that as I have watched over them to pluck up, to break down, to throw down, to destroy, and to afflict, so I will watch over them to build and to plant. . . .

Behold, the days are coming, says the LORD, when I will make a new covenant . . . not according to the covenant I made with their fathers. . . . This is the covenant that I will make with the house of Israel. . . . I will put My law in their minds, and write it on their hearts; and I will be their God, and they shall be My people."

Once Jeremiah staked his claim on the future, it really didn't matter that there was darkness that would attempt to overcome his land—because God had a plan. If we trust Him in the midst of our warfare and obey Him to do the faith acts He requires of us, God will secure our future even in the midst of war. Jeremiah 33:3 says, "Call to Me and I will answer you and show you great and mighty things, fenced in and hidden, which you do not know (do not distinguish and recognize, have knowledge of and understand)" (AMPC). Because God has a great future for us, we can shout loudly and get His attention in the midst of our warfare so that He shows us things we could not normally see. In the midst of whatever haziness presents itself in the now, He will show us our future. Most of us are used to watching out for what we presently have and what is dear to us. But we must also watch after our future.

We can neither watch *after* nor *for* the future if we are not exhibiting the presence of the Lord from our abiding place. It is His presence that allows us to see into our future. Sadly, many Christians get nervous when talking about seeing into the future. We give this the same stigma associated with fortune-tellers and palm readers. Let me say this as clearly as I know how: God's people must have foresight! We must have vision for what lies ahead, or we will be unprepared. And in these times, preparation and readiness are essential.

Heaven's View of the Horizon

We must see from heaven and walk in the world around us. We must know our place in the world, but live from our positional abiding place of eternity. We must never forget that we have a horizon line in the overall picture of our timeline in the earth that is beyond the day we are trudging through. You have a future and a hope. Never lose sight of heaven's overall plan for your life. Without maintaining this vision, we perish—go backward and never meet the goal of the time in the earth that we were meant to occupy.

I have always been an irregular sleeper. Some people use the term "light sleeper," but that doesn't exactly fit me. I've never developed good sleep patterns because of the turmoil and trauma that I grew up in. This has had some negative effects on my health, but on the positive side, it's also allowed me to commune with the Lord and keep watch while most people are fast asleep. I'll never forget one night in particular.

Pam had gone to bed at our normal time of eleven o'clock, but I continued to stay up to read the Bible and pray. I was immersed in the Word, having a wonderful time with the Lord, when I suddenly felt the Spirit of God come down into the room of our home where I was praying. His presence was tangible. I then heard His voice say an interesting thing to me: *You can turn Satan into his own fire. When his fiery darts come against you, repel those darts and return them against him.*

Like most anyone would have reacted in that same situation, I was a little stunned. I wasn't exactly sure what God's words meant, but I knew by the Spirit that they had done something within me. At the time, Pam and I were seeing great breakthroughs in our lives personally and in other areas in which we were seeking Him. I had been praying for lost people in our church and they were getting saved. I was being favored in the workplace. Overall, I was learning to prevail in prayer. So even though I wasn't too sure about the meaning of God's words, I knew for certain that He would reveal what I needed to know in time. At about two in the morning, I turned off the lights and went to bed.

Only an hour later, Pam and I were suddenly awakened by our dog, Josh, who had jumped into bed with us and was yapping as if there were a burglar in the house. We sat up and discovered the real source of distress: Standing next to our bed was a presence! To me, the presence had a distinct physical form, dressed like a woman with a man's voice. Pam, however, saw it differently. She said it was a green-like slime form with fiery eyes. (Looking back, this is yet another reminder of how most of us see into the spirit realm but perceive things differently, even though what we perceive is actually the same.)

Almost immediately I said, "Who are you and what gives you the right to be here?"

"I am Ashteroth," the presence replied, "and I have come to take your children." Not your average houseguest, that's for sure!

At that moment, Pam and I had the choice to be gripped with fear over this visitor's presence and its menacing words, or turn to the Lord. We chose His truth. I instantly stood up and said, "In the name of Jesus, you have to leave this house!" Pam and I then began to clap and shout, overwhelmed with joy.

You see, up to that point in our lives, we were barren. We had been seeking God for children but were unable to conceive. It was disheartening, yet we trusted the Lord. This force had come and announced the will of darkness to take our children. But instead of us falling to the ploy of the enemy and submitting in fear and confusion, we rejoiced. Why would we be happy over this presence? Because what this evil force was really announcing was that we were going to have children! Yes, there would be a war over the children, but I knew the Lord well enough to know that once we had children I could trust Him to keep what He had blessed us with.

There was another element to this encounter that dramatically changed our lives. When I commanded this force to leave our house, I was also declaring that any familial spirit that had been in our bloodlines and had been sent against us would now have to fully let go and remove itself from our sphere of authority. The change was instant—as crazy as it sounds, the room actually lit up. God's presence so flooded our bedroom that it became as bright as day. When we resisted evil, His glory came in and overtook our atmosphere.

The incident that night revealed a level of warfare we had never been in before, but that was not the most important thing. The main point was that God's manifest presence was now free to rule this particular area of our lives. And what was revealed was a truth that is key to this chapter: Once evil is confronted in our atmosphere, then God's presence has the liberty to replace evil with glory.

Pam and I were in a fierce presence-and-glory war in that scenario, yet in the midst of our conflict with the enemy, we found out even more about God's good plan for our future—that we would have children. Heaven's view of the horizon was very different from the earthly view. The enemy's dark plan to steal, kill, and destroy could not overcome God's plan for our future and our hope!

When Pam and I had our encounter with the enemy's forces that night, it left us with a vision for the future. We knew that what the enemy had planned for harm, God meant for good (see Exodus 50:20). And so we began to cry out for our children. Two years later, we received our first child, Daniel. Two years after that, Pam was healed and we conceived our second child, Rebekah. From then on, several other children and many grandchildren were to come forth.

One of the primary reasons God allows us to see into the future is for the benefit of the generations who are arising. We must prepare the way for God's best in the lives of those who will follow. The Lord doesn't give us glimpses just to titillate us or make us long for better days ahead. The vision of God—which we all need—always has a divine purpose.

Another reason God supplies prophetic vision, one we've already hinted at, is simply for strategy. We cannot be victorious against the forces of darkness that rule our world without the precise, perfect plans of the Lord. Here are some directives that I believe are important for each of us to trust the Lord for in the days ahead:

1. *Ask for three generations to agree prophetically over what God has said.* This reflects the tri-generational nature of our God—that He was the God of Abraham, Isaac and Jacob. It also aligns with Isaiah 59:21, where we find God pronouncing a covenant that His word will be in the mouths of three generations. When this happens, He will unlock the heavens and manifest His presence in the earth.

2. *Trust that He will expand your borders and redefine your sphere of authority.* When this happens, you will see people running to find out what you are about. The Lord will secure your inheritance of souls won for Him. There came a time when Naomi said to Ruth, "Daughter, how shall I secure your inheritance? Not only do you have a future, but you can begin now to secure it!" (see Ruth 3:1–4).

3. *See your storehouse as full.* Before you can do that, however, you must *define your storehouse.* What areas of provision has God established in your life? Let Him show them to you, and ask Him how to fill them. He will give you the strategy.

4. *Don't allow your past to rule you.* God can take situations from the past and bring them into the present so that you

can reconcile your own mistakes and failures. When your past is reconciled, your future is unlocked.

5. *Believe that you can defeat your enemy!* See your enemy. See his headship broken over your life. Do not be afraid to discover how his voice has ruled your bloodline. Remember Jesus! The cross broke the headship of Satan. Drive a stake through his headship and you will begin to hear what God has for your future.

6. *Never forget that you have been given the ability to connect heaven and earth.* Let the Lord teach you to pray today, "Thy will in heaven, come to earth!"

7. *Watch for your divine connections.* They are on your path already. Success means that the Lord has positioned help on the way ahead. When you see a divine connection that God has placed on your path, watch Him develop that covenant relationship to help you establish your future.

These seven points are crucial to our success in the coming wars. They also emphasize the need for God's presence to be stronger than ever in our lives. Remember, when we establish His presence, we force out every power of darkness. His glory always overcomes!

War in the Atmosphere

Understanding the natural concept of the earth's atmosphere will help us understand the spiritual atmosphere we're living in, where a war is being fought over God's presence and the reflection of His glory. The *American Dictionary of the English Language* defines the *atmosphere* as the whole mass of fluid, consisting of air, aqueous and other vapors, that surrounds the earth.[1] This word is rooted in the interaction between vapor and the earth's sphere. Vapor encompasses this sphere we live on and consists of a moist, floating substance like an invisible, elastic fluid. The Bible refers to this when it says, "Certainly every man at his best state is but vapor" (Psalm 39:5 NKJV). When we speak of "the atmosphere," however, we're often referring to a generic sense of the airborne aura surrounding us. The atmosphere affects everything it surrounds, and changes in the atmosphere do the same.

What does the atmosphere have to do with a war over God's presence? Actually, everything. We have an atmosphere about us that affects the way the earth operates. The atmosphere we carry affects the land we walk on. The more we are in union with God and His purpose for the earth, the more we create a right atmosphere around us.

To usher in God's presence requires a change in the atmosphere, and we are assigned the task of bringing this about! The Bible establishes that Satan is the god of this world, the "prince of the power of the air" (Ephesians 2:2 NKJV). Yet how is this so if Psalm 24:1 (NKJV) says, "The earth is the LORD's, and all its fullness"? First, we must understand the terms used in those two verses. The Greek word for "earth" is *topos*, while the word for "world" is *cosmos*. This means that any structure that protrudes or is above the *topos* is subject to warfare. Second, we must realize the Bible establishes that there are three heavens. God and all His heavenly beings dwell in the third heaven. Satan, as the ruler of the air, attempts to rule from the second heaven to illegally legislate in the first heaven—that place where we physically stand above the earth.

Apostle Kim Daniels, in her book *Give It Back*, explains it this way:

> Ephesians 2:2 describes the assignment of the prince of the power of the air. One name for the Greek god of the second heaven is Zeus. The second heaven is the demonic headquarters that is strategically set up to control people like puppets on a string. In the spirit, that is exactly how it looks—like a puppet show! Every human being

is connected to either the second or third heaven. People who are bound by second heaven activity are connected to the second heaven by demonic strings.

The hydra is the god of recurring curses and is also seated in the heavens. It is one of the constellations or groups of stars that abide in the heavens. The power of the air (or unconscious cycles) is a subliminal bondage, which is controlled from the air. This spirit hides behind the cover of natural habits, and its victims never suspect that they are under its control. Before people are delivered from addictions and habits, demonic strings must be cut in the spirit to sever their alliances with the second heaven. After this, ground-level deliverance can take place.[2]

We must determine who is in charge and ruling in our atmosphere. Are we going to legislate God's rule in our atmosphere or will our enemy control it? This is one of our greatest warfare dynamics to understand. In *Authority in Prayer*, Dutch Sheets writes:

> Where God and Satan are concerned, the issue has never been power, including control of the earth. God is all-powerful. . . . It is always and only a question of authority.
>
> The same is true with us and our struggle with the kingdom of darkness. Satan didn't gain any power at the Fall and didn't lose any at the cross. His power or ability didn't change at either event. His authority, or the right to use his power, did. In fact, though Christians often state otherwise, Scripture nowhere says that Christ delivered us from or dealt with Satan's power at Calvary. He dealt with Satan's authority.[3]

We must learn to legislate our realm of authority, while understanding that it is not the same thing as wielding power. Our realm of authority includes both heaven and earth. That is what makes up our atmosphere. Jesus broke Satan's headship and removed his legal authority at the cross. He then overcame death, hell, and the grave. He liberated the captives. However, we must keep Satan's power neutralized and defeated in the place in the earth where God has called us to be His stewards. That is what Elijah did when he commanded the heavens to withhold rain for three and a half years (see 1 Kings 17). Then, knowing it was God's perfect time for rain, he birthed a cloud into his atmosphere. The atmosphere was then filled with rain.

Is a Curse Working in Your Midst?

Satan has a million different ways in which he tries to extend his dominion of the air. This chapter is not dedicated to identifying all those opposing tactics, but I do feel it necessary to highlight one in particular: curses. Passed down through time, curses work with iniquitous patterns that have developed in our bloodline. Let's look at how curses play a major role in our reclaiming the atmosphere around us.

Though it seems almost too simple, one of the ways that you can detect a curse is by recognizing the absence of God's glory or presence. According to *The Encyclopedia of Jewish Myth, Magic and Mysticism*, a curse is a "verbal invocation to bring harm, evil or detriment on another. More than a threat or a wish, a curse is assumed to have the power to make the desired harm a reality."[4] Curses result from not hearing God's voice or from receiving another voice that is contrary to God's plan for your life. Curses will agree with internal deficiencies within us such as rebellion, lust, or any other sin of the flesh. Derek Prince wrote a wonderful book called *Blessing or Curse: You Can Choose*. In his analysis of Deuteronomy 28, he says there are seven main categories that curses deal with:

1. Mental and/or emotional breakdown
2. Repeated or chronic sicknesses (especially if hereditary)

3. Barrenness, a tendency to miscarry, or related female problems

4. Breakdown of marriage or family alienation

5. Continuing financial insufficiency

6. Being "accident-prone"

7. A history of suicides and unnatural or untimely deaths[5]

The cycles of hell want to weigh you down and keep you from abiding! Because I teach so much on breaking old cycles, I want to be sure that you recognize that curses can be timed and sequenced so that they reoccur from generation to generation. This will continue to take place until the iniquitous pattern in a bloodline or the iniquitous violation on a piece of land has been addressed. I have much experience with both of these patterns. In fact, my wife jokes that I'm qualified to teach on demonic powers all over the world because my family had all of them in operation! Many of those curses operated on the land that we owned. I won't tell all of those stories here, but I will say this: The Lord took me through a forty-year process going back and forth to places where iniquitous defilements occurred in our family. He then would have me repent and release His presence to replace the working of evil. I read many books on cleansing the land and discovered that there are four major areas of iniquity that cause curses to have a right to operate in a land: covenant breaking, idolatry or blood sacrifice, illegal bloodshed, and sexual immorality.

Many Christian leaders make light of the concept of curses. I do not want to do that. I do believe that curses are conditional. I am well aware that they can come through words, timing, and astrological influences, or magical incantations and actions. More importantly, however, curses can be broken.

A man once approached me who was from a denominational background. The group he worked with had bought a new piece of land to build a school and ministry on. When he and some of his coworkers were walking on the land, they got to a place where everyone immediately sensed a change in the atmosphere. Every hair on his body seemed to stand up. He asked me what that meant.

"When that happens, it means you have discerned a presence of evil," I answered. "It is the Holy Spirit manifesting in you with the gift of discerning evil spirits." He then asked me what he should do and how he should pray. I said, "Well, first of all, you pray until all the hair on your body goes down! That means you have commanded the presence of evil to let go of the place where you are standing and the atmosphere has been cleansed." The group later found several places where satanic sacrifices had been made on their land.

Planning for the Presence

We need to stay seated and rule from our abiding place, and allow God's glory and presence to permeate both the earthen realm's land and the atmosphere we walk in. This is what the Lord told Joshua—*If you will meditate day and night on what I have said, every place your foot sets I will give you* (see Joshua 1).

Many of us need to reclaim territories just as this group did. While this can certainly involve claiming victory over the dark history behind a piece of physical land, more often than not it involves cleaning out areas of our lives in which God's glory is not fully seen. We must become people of His presence, consumed with His habitation throughout every inch of our atmosphere.

King David was such a person. Despite making some major mistakes during his reign, David loved the presence of God and had a heart that was turned after God. He was always willing to rely on God to salvage his failures and restore him.

In 2 Samuel 6, we find an account of how David first attempted to bring the Ark of the Covenant into Jerusalem, where he lived. His desire was pure: He wanted the presence of God to surround his life. Yet his execution was flawed and left one of his men dead. As a result,

David feared transporting the Ark to his house and instead left it at the home of Obed-Edom. Scripture says, "And the Lord blessed Obed-Edom and all his household," and this was relayed to David.

What is interesting is that this Hebrew word for "blessed" is *barak*, which at its root means "to kneel." Jeff A. Benner, on his Ancient Hebrew Research Center website, gives an understanding of this word as, "Yahweh (he who exists) will kneel before you presenting gifts."[6] The Ark was only with Obed-Edom for three months, yet there was a discernible change in his situation that caused others to recognize that he was being blessed, that Yahweh was presenting him with gifts—all because of the presence of the Ark!

The mistake wasn't in David's heart or in his lack of preparation. David had already built a site for the Ark. He had established a special place for God's presence to dwell. No, the lesson David learned was simply this: *How we invite the presence of God and how we honor His presence are very important.* David serves as a wonderful example because although he made a great mistake, he discovered how to properly bring the Ark to the City of David. According to Matthew Easton in the *Bible Encyclopedia*, he then entered a "series of conquests which greatly extended and strengthened his kingdom (2 Samuel 8). In a few years, the whole territory from the Euphrates to the river of Egypt, and from Gaza on the west to Thapsacus on the east, was under his sway (2 Samuel 8:3–13; 10)."[7]

According to Leen and Kathleen Ritmeyer in *From Sinai to Jerusalem: The Wanderings of the Holy Ark*, the Ark was placed right next to David's palace, in his yard.[8] Living on his property, *in his backyard*, was the God who brought him gifts! The Tabernacle of David would have remained there for about thirty years. I believe this is what gave David great credibility in war. What an incredible principle! When we have the presence of God in our homes, the gifts of God are bestowed abundantly on our lives and we are successful in war.

However, I also believe therefore David was judged so severely when he didn't go to war and fell into passivity, lust, manipulation, and murder after coveting Bathsheba. When we commit open sin while in God's presence, our problems escalate. This is why it is more disastrous when a minister hides a lifestyle of sin than for an everyday Christian to do so. Obviously, sin is sin, but the influence that we have from the presence of God in our midst is not to be taken lightly. I believe we are more accountable when we are aware of God's presence in our midst and we do not act accordingly.

John Dickson, a fellow minister and friend of mine who co-authored *The Worship Warrior* with me, writes the following about David in a personal communication:

What was unique about the Tabernacle of David was that it was a heavenly paradigm in an earthly setting. When David brought in the Ark, there was already a Tabernacle specifically designed to house it: The tabernacle of Moses was just down the road in Gibeon (see 2 Chron. 1:4–5). But God said of David that He would "carry out My program fully" (Acts 13:22, AMP) and so we find David setting up a different kind of tent on Zion's hill with no brazen altar, no laver, no lampstand, no altar of incense, no table of show bread and—most importantly—no veil. The worshippers entered the very presence of God face-to-face, just like they did in heaven. The way they worshipped was also just like in heaven: With no forms or rituals, they sang and danced and prophesied and warred before the Lord as the minions of heaven are seen doing in the book of Revelation.

There in that Tabernacle on Zion's hill, God enthroned Himself on their praises (see Ps. 22:3) and from that throne He stretched forth His scepter (see Ps. 110:1–3), issued His commands (see Ps. 133:3), declared His blessings (see Ps. 128:5; 134:3), heard the prayers of the destitute (see Ps. 102:17) and punished His enemies (see Isa. 66:6). That word *enthroned* implies in the Hebrew that God not only came to sit as judge, but also to stay or to dwell—even to marry. God was not going to leave once His "work" was done. He had found a suitable dwelling place for His presence to continually dwell on earth. Psalm 132 says "For the LORD has chosen Zion; He has desired it for His habitation. This is My resting place forever; here I will dwell, for I have desired it" (Ps. 132:13–14, NASB). In David's Tabernacle, God was in the midst of continual praises. It was just like His holy hill, by the same name, in heaven. As a matter of fact, Psalm 78 says that God built His sanctuary on Mount Zion "like the heights" (Ps. 78:67–69) or just like it was built in heaven. God's presence, which was continually manifested in heaven, was now continually manifested on the earth. His people could come into that small tent and experience that presence just like the inhabitants of heaven. How wonderful!⁹

Throughout the Bible, we see that God is enthroned in praise. We glorify Him through our worship. We ascend to our heavenly position when we worship. That is why praise and worship are essential to experiencing God's glory. Praise is that element of celebration that can transport us into the throne room of God. God comes down with us and inhabits our praises. Once we are in the throne room at His feet, the only suitable response is to worship and adore Him. As we worship Him in that intimate place, He begins to reveal His glory to us. God is looking for true worshipers who will worship "in the Spirit and in truth" (John 4:24), and as He finds those worshipers, they are able to experience the reality of heaven, which is God's glory.

The Lights Went Out, But the Lamp Was Lit!

Throughout the Bible, God's glory is often seen in terms of radiant light. In his well-known introduction, Gospel-writer John describes Christ as "the true Light which gives light to every man coming into the world" (1:9 NKJV). In Revelation, the same apostle describes the New Jerusalem as having "no need of the sun or of the moon to shine in it, for the glory of God illuminated it. The Lamb is its light" (21:23 NKJV). Jesus declared Himself "the light of the world" (John 8:12).

What is often just as interesting to me is that Christ crowned those of us who follow Him with the very same title. In Matthew 5:14–15, He said of believers, "You are the light of the world. A city that is set on a hill cannot be hidden. Nor do they light a lamp and put it under a basket, but on a lampstand, and it gives light to all who are in the house." In the remainder of this chapter, I want to delve into the deeper meaning of this vivid imagery of lights and lampstands. Allow me to start by offering a wonderful illustration of the importance God places on His Son—and us—being the light of the world.

I travel all over the country and usually find myself in Houston several times a year. In November 2002, I was ministering at the Worship Convivium in Houston, hosted by Lora Allison. I had been sharing a message on my heart from Jeremiah 1:11–12, which is part of Jeremiah's initiation as a watchman prophet. In those verses, the Lord asks Jeremiah an important question: *What do you see?* This would be crucial to our meetings that week.

Friday morning when we came to the meeting, I shared with Lora that I felt the Lord was going to do something new and we would have to follow Him to experience what He wanted. After the first song in worship, I felt I was to stand up and give a teaching instruction over what God was saying and how it related to what we were singing. I then made a declaration that God was going to transform Houston, but it would be in His way.

I sat down after about fifteen minutes of speaking and we started to worship again. Suddenly, the whole place went pitch black, with no electricity for instruments, lights, sound, or anything else plugged in. (A transformer had blown in the Houston area where we were having the meeting.) Almost immediately the Lord said, *Let Me lead you into the sound I have.*

I stood up and asked the question to the whole group: "What do you see?" Of course, we saw darkness. Then someone brought in a lampstand or menorah with seven candles lit. I responded by saying to the Lord, "Lord, I see your lampstand in the midst of the darkness."

So the Lord said, *Yes, darkness is coming upon the earth, but I am lighting a lamp in the midst of the darkness. This will be a season where those with My light will shine brightly. This will also be a season of removing. I will remove My lampstand from certain churches, cities, states, and nations.*

I went on and prophesied for another hour. During this time, God added each sound that He wanted to bring forth. It was one of the most incredible gatherings I've ever been in. It was as if the whole place knew when to dance. The violin knew exactly when to play, the drums when to beat, the horns when to resound, and the singers when to come out front and sing prophetically. It was definitely a "transforming" time.

Yet the words we received that day still ring true today: The Lord will continue to move us out of the soulish realm of worship that we are presently operating in. The methods and mindsets concerning worship are changing. And in the midst of our darkness, the Lord will send forth the light that will guide us.

Stay Abiding as War Comes

Stay abiding as war comes into your atmosphere. The Body of Christ is living in an intense season of warfare. My son, Daniel, recently spoke on "The War for Our Inheritance." There are wars over our minds, our blood, our time, our land, the nations we live in, and our future. These wars occur in our atmosphere. Will the forces of darkness occupy our territories, or will God's glory finally flood the earth?

Sadly, the Body of Christ is also in a place of frustration. We have the appearance of getting many things accomplished, yet in reality we are not getting anything done because things are changing so quickly. Our busyness, if we do not keep it in check, is crowding out our efforts to see God's presence established in our territories.

On an individual level, it has become more difficult to find our abiding place in Him because people keep interrupting our time of preparation.

This season, I see the glory of God getting released in the marketplace before He manifests Himself in the Church. We have not defined our harvest fields, nor have we gathered the harvest that is before us. Therefore, the enemy is attacking the harvest field. The current Body of Christ, as well as its leadership, must gather with an understanding of the atmosphere around us. We must recognize both the harvest fields in our reach and how the war is escalating in our midst.

I believe that the leaders of today's Church are now hearing the call of heaven to rally the Body in prayer—because they know the war that is at hand! They know we must be prepared! They also know we must define our harvest fields and have a plan to gather the harvest that is before us.

To accomplish what God has for us and reveal His glory on the earth, we must understand the atmospheric war that surrounds us. The Lord is telling those who are His prophetic watchmen for this hour to be a protection to the present gathering. We must stand watch in His perfect timing, awaiting His signal. And when we see those forces approaching, we must cry loudly, signaling the battle cry, so that the Body will be alerted to the war in the harvest fields.

It all comes down to staking our claim in our abiding place, thus winning the presence-and-glory war in the atmosphere of the heavenlies. Stay seated there! Stay abiding in His presence! Rule!

QUESTIONS FOR ABIDING DEEPER

- What does "staking your claim from your abiding place" mean to you now that you have read this chapter?

- When was the last time you sensed God's presence in your atmosphere? If you have never sensed His presence, ask Him now to reveal His glory to you.
- In the midst of the presence-and-glory war, how does abiding in His presence help you gain wisdom from heaven into any situation you must face on earth?

18

ABIDE AND BE TRANSFORMED

Chuck D. Pierce

Surrounded then as we are by these serried ranks of witnesses, let us strip off everything that hinders us, as well as the sin which dogs our feet, and let us run the race that we have to run with patience, our eyes fixed on Jesus the source and the goal of our faith. For he himself endured.

Hebrews 12:1–2 PHILLIPS

Run the race you were meant to run! Abide! Stay focused! Rejoice! *Seek the Kingdom first!*

Don't just dwell on you, "your four and nothing more." Enjoy life. Don't let the cares of the world produce anxiety in you. Weights and anxiety can make us earthbound. Instead, learn the art of meditation on God and His Word. Live a *zoe* life—the Greek word used to express the life Jesus gives His followers—a life filled with power and energy! Stay disciplined!

In *Possessing Your Inheritance* (Chosen, 2009), Rebecca Wagner Sytsema and I write about spiritual discipline. Discipline and love work together to keep us buoyant in faith and floating above the chaos of the world.

Many Christians don't understand the need for personal disciplines like prayer, fasting, meditating on the Word, giving, work, rest, etc. Therefore, they don't abide in the dwelling place God has prepared for them. Discipline is key to preventing the enemy from stealing your inheritance. It is key to keeping the "spiritual life" process flowing in you. Ask God to give you a plan to develop any disciplines in which you may be weak.

Feast on the Word

The key to overcoming and to having success is meditation on God and His Word. Chew on your revelation. Feast on the Word. Succeed! Conquest your promise! Entering into a promise God has given you is one thing, but it's another dimension to *conquest* in that promise and secure what He has spoken to you.

> This Book of the Law shall not depart from your mouth, but you shall meditate in it day and night, that you may observe to do according to all that is written in it. For then you will make your way prosperous, and then you will have good success.
>
> Joshua 1:8 NKJV

One of the ways God has provided for our success is contingent on our willingness to take time to meditate on His Word. Why? Because if we just read God's Word without taking time to give it thought, we deny ourselves the opportunity to receive personal revelation, refreshment for our soul and spirit, and increased understanding in order to align ourselves with God's will in prayer. Pastor and author

Donald S. Whitney puts it this way in his book *Spiritual Disciplines for the Christian Life*:

> Meditation is the missing link between Bible intake and prayer. . . .
> There should be a smooth, almost unnoticeable transition between
> Scripture input and prayer output so that we move even closer to
> God in those moments. This happens when there is the link of medi-
> tation in between.[1]

Meditation is actually synonymous with a cow chewing its cud. The cow will eat some food and then later bring it back up and chew on it again and again, until the food finally becomes part of that cow's being. Many times when God speaks to us, we are in awe and have no clue how God will accomplish what He has spoken. Mary pondered—meditated on—what the Holy Spirit spoke to her about the birth of Jesus. It became part of her, until she brought that word to birth and watched the Word made flesh grow to maturity and into the fullness of God's plan. We need to be like Mary and allow God's Word to become part of us.

The problem is simply a matter of patience. I have found that as a whole, our society is very impatient. Add to that the nonstop hectic schedules most people face, and there seems little time for quality meditation. We must repent before God for not following the command to meditate day and night, and ask Him to break the power of impatience from us. Once that happens and we learn the discipline of meditation, we'll find that we are willing to wait on God until we hear from Him concerning our circumstances.

Focus on God, not Distractions

Stay focused, and don't get distracted. Choose to be like Mary of Bethany. Don't get weighed down by your earthly duties, like Mary's sister, Martha. Focus on God's purpose instead. When Jesus had arrived and been welcomed at their home, He told Martha she was distracted (not abiding). Meanwhile, Mary sat at His feet and listened to His word. She stayed focused on the highest purpose of the moment.

Martha, however, became "distracted with much serving" (Luke 10:40 NKJV). The word *distracted* in Greek is *perispao*, which means to be encumbered and dragged all around.[2] Martha even approached Jesus and said, "Lord, do you not care that my sister has left me to serve alone?" (verse 40 NKJV). In other words, Martha was telling Jesus, "Make my sister come drag around in circles with me!"

Jesus responded, "Martha, Martha, you are worried and troubled about many things. But one thing is needed, and Mary has chosen that good part, which will not be taken away from her" (verses 41–42 NKJV).

This is a time in history when the events occurring around us can distract us from the highest purpose of God. With so much to deal with in our daily lives, and with all the cares of the world, it's easy to become "worried and troubled about many things." In the Greek, the word for *worry* is *merimnaó*, which means "divided into parts."[3] This word can also suggest a distraction or preoccupation with things that cause anxiety, stress, and pressure. It means straying from a focused goal we are called to accomplish. In Matthew 6:25–30 (NKJV), Jesus states,

> Therefore I say to you, do not worry about your life, what you will eat or what you will drink; nor about your body, what you will put on. Is not life more than food and the body more than clothing? Look at the birds of the air. . . . Are you not of more value than they? . . .
>
> So why do you worry about clothing? Consider the lilies of the field, how they grow: they neither toil nor spin; and yet I say to you that even Solomon in all his glory was not arrayed like one of these. Now if God so clothes the grass of the field, which today is, and tomorrow is thrown into the oven, will He not much more clothe you, O you of little faith?

Distraction and worry can fragment us. Martha was proud of her home and glad to have the Lord visiting, but she missed the purpose of His visit. Jesus wasn't there on a social visit. He was there to release His word to the city of Bethany. Mary's focus and attention enabled her to perceive the best that was yet ahead for her life. Martha's distraction put her in danger of missing the best that God had for her. She became distracted and preoccupied instead of taking the opportunity to gain necessary revelation for her future.

We must work when God says work, but we need to be intimate when we have the opportunity to be intimate. Whatever we are doing, we must always stay focused and avoid becoming distracted.

Stay in God's Timing

Be at the right place at the right time. Stay in God's timing. Let's continue following the story of Mary and Martha's relationship with Jesus. These sisters encounter a terrible crisis when their brother, Lazarus, becomes ill. They've seen Jesus' power in the past, so they ask Him to come visit Lazarus, saying, "Lord, behold, he whom You love is sick" (John 11:3 NKJV).

When Jesus heard this, He said, "This sickness is not unto death, but for the glory of God" (verse 4 NKJV). We are told that Jesus loved Mary, Martha, and Lazarus, yet when He heard that Lazarus was sick, He stayed two more days where He was (see verses 5–6). So many times when we are in terrible circumstances, we forget the Lord's love for us. Other times when we are asking Him to fulfill a desire of our heart and He says *Wait*, we lose sight of His faithfulness to us.

Jesus couldn't be coerced out of His Father's timing in this scenario. He always watched for key *opportune times* to reflect the Father's glory from heaven. Even though Jesus loved this family, He didn't immediately leave His post to visit His sick friend. Instead, He waited two days. His delay meant that Lazarus was in the grave for four days. According to the beliefs of the time, this meant that Lazarus was good and dead and that his soul had departed.

This event revealed Jesus' ability to control His emotions. Even friends and close acquaintances couldn't coerce Him out of the Father's timing. He wasn't moved to action by external forces. This is a key principle for us to remember in the days ahead. We must control our emotions to keep ourselves in God's perfect timing, and to ensure that we will be at the right place at the right time.

Jesus also chose the key place to address the "strong man" of unbelief. In John 11:7, Jesus told His disciples that it was now time to visit Judea. Bethany, where Lazarus and his sisters resided, was a gateway into Judea, a stronghold of religion and unbelief. Yet it was in this same atmosphere that Jesus preformed the powerful miracle of raising Lazarus from the dead. I believe our most difficult war is to remain in our abiding place and address unbelief. Unbelief is such a hindering force that it can keep us from seeing the best that God has for us in days ahead.

Finally, Jesus revealed the progression of faith necessary to be overcomers. Jesus kept working with Martha, Mary, and His disciples to show them His character. He encouraged them to believe: "If you would believe," He kept saying, "you would see the glory of God" (John 11:40; see also verses 15, 26). Our faith level must be raised to a new dimension in the Body of Christ to overcome what's ahead. Resurrection, life, and faith have a proportionate relationship, which is necessary for us to understand if we are to overcome what's ahead in our future. Jesus turned hopelessness into resurrection power. Martha and Mary had lost all hope of seeing their brother again. However, Jesus kept breaking the power of hopelessness and encouraging them in faith. We must be delivered from hope deferred now!

To *resurrect* means to bring to view, to attention, or to use again. It also means to raise from the dead or raise again to life. Why did John devote so much time to recording this particular miracle? Was the raising of a dead person the issue? What was the relationship of this particular display of power and the events that were to come? Jesus stated that Lazarus's sickness was not unto death, but for the glory of God. This was a culminating event in Jesus' life that preceded His Triumphal Entry, His death, and His ultimate defeat of the dark powers holding humanity. Jesus overcame and was resurrected, and in doing so, He defeated hopelessness in our lives.

Abide, and Recover All

Jesus' shout of "*Come forth!*" created a recovery. Lazarus was brought back to life when Jesus shouted, "Lazarus, come forth!" (John 11:43 NKJV).

This is a season of recovery in the Body of Christ, too. Hear the Lord shouting over you, "*Come forth!*" The Hebrew word for this means we must escape, break out, bring forth, draw to an end, lead out, or depart from a condemned situation.[4] Let this shout of the Lord rise in your midst and declare a recovery of what you've lost in the past season.

Here's a list of areas over which you can proclaim this super-natural recovery in your life, along with Scriptures to use to declare victory in each area:

- Recover lost and broken relationships (see Genesis 45).
- Recover your prophetic call (see Psalm 105:17–22).
- Recover delayed promises (see 2 Corinthians 1:20).
- Recover the spirit and gift of faith (see Psalm 23:3; Romans 1:17).
- Recover the miracle of healing (see Jeremiah 30:17).
- Recover your spiritual stability (see 1 Samuel 7:11–14; 2 Chronicles 20:6).
- Recover your financial stability (see Malachi 3:10).

- Recover joy (see Nehemiah 8:10).
- Recover wasted years (see Joel 2:25).
- Recover lost sheep stolen from your pasture (see 1 Samuel 17:34–37; 30:20).
- Recover the blessings of God (see Deuteronomy 28:1–4; Proverbs 3:33).
- Recover all (see 1 Samuel 30:8).

Keep Your Fire Burning

Keep your fire burning! John the Baptist cried in the desert, "I baptize you with water for repentance, but after me comes one who is more powerful than I. . . . He will baptize you with the Holy Spirit and fire" (Matthew 3:11).

We must understand that we have to know this fire and keep it burning within us in order to experience a perpetual relationship with God—and a move of God within and around us. The fire of God is a sign of spiritual renewal, consecration, and empowerment.

In modern history, we have forgotten the importance of God's altar. In our previous book *Rekindle the Altar Fire* (Chosen, 2020), Alemu and I wrote a modern-day explanation of the altar. We gave a call for us as God's people to find our way back to building His altar, which results in experiencing His fire, joy, and renewal. That book will help you learn much about worship and will motivate you to "go up to a high place," tear down the devil's altar, and build God's altar.

Now is the time for our generation to build God's altar so that His fire may fall. *Build now! Your future depends on the altar.*

Resting Makes the Top 10!

Shabbat Shalom! Rest in God! Abide in Him! God labored six days, and then He rested on the seventh. In the Ten Commandments, He commanded us to do the same.

Rest must be a big issue in order to make the Top 10 in God's commands![5] There are several reasons why. First, rest is a matter of obedience to God. He commanded us to rest. The children of Israel learned this lesson the hard way when, because of their unwillingness to observe God's Sabbath command, they were sent into captivity in Babylon.

Second, rest is an issue of trust in God. Cindy Jacobs expounds on this:

> *Vine's Old Testament* concordance says that by resting, man witnessed his trust in God to give fruit to his labor. Perhaps when we continue to work without time off, we are saying to God, "You cannot bless the fruit of my labor if I take time out" (or) "I have to do this even if it breaks down my physical body, or causes harm to my loved ones" (or) "There is no one but me who can do what I do."[6]

Now, most of us would state up front that we don't believe these things. Yet our actions belie this.

The third and perhaps most obvious reason for resting is that it promotes our physical well-being. God knows how He created us and how much physical rest we need. We must rest to gain the new strength we need for what lies ahead. An extra cup of coffee in the morning will *not* accomplish the same thing!

The Sabbath rest means to stop, cease, or end and meditate on the glories of God's creation, which is a fourth reason to rest. Cindy Jacobs goes on to share,

> One aspect of the Sabbath was that it was to be a day or season of reflecting on God, who He is and what He has done for us in all of His fullness. This is a powerful concept. Rest is not complete without time to reflect on the Lord.[7]

Such rest and reflection are what Psalm 23:2 (NLT) refers to: "He lets me rest in green meadows; he leads me beside peaceful streams."

Abiding in His Presence

This is a picture of stillness and meditation. In this time of pause and quietness, we reflect. We look back and develop course corrections, and we look forward and strategize concerning our path ahead.

Abide, and Be Transformed

Every question demands a response. Let your faith act. *Doing reinforces hearing.* Moving by faith will tear down old mindsets that would hinder us in the future. Think differently. Watch your prayer life change as you dialogue with the Lord in a new and different way each day.

When we examine the teachings and ministry of Jesus, isn't it interesting that He, having all knowledge as the Son of God, chose to ask questions rather than just supply all the answers? The Lord asks us questions to cause us to think differently and critically. He stirs our minds and prompts us so that we will seek His way.

Our hearts and minds are being stirred to ask a question that echoes the one Jesus asked His disciples in Matthew 16:15: "Who do you say I am?" God is still demanding a response today to each question He asks, and to each thought we have that exalts our way of thinking above His. This is what makes Him so real. The Lord has never ceased interacting with His people. What He desires is a people who are willing to gather His thoughts above their own, assess His ways, and then align with His strategies.

Abide, and Think Like Him

The essence of critical thinking for the astute believer is *abiding and aligning with God's thoughts.* To dismantle a stronghold, we must go through the process of realigning the way we think. There are steps each of us can take. We must sharpen our mind, develop critical thinking skills, and capture our thoughts.

Contrary to popular belief, you can teach an old dog new tricks. I am living proof of this! Several years ago, the Lord visited me while I was in my office, preparing to speak at our church's Feast of Tabernacles celebration. He said, *In these critical times, you must think critically.*

The statement left a profound mark on me. I knew a few things about the process of critical thinking. However, there was a new depth that the Lord was intending to teach me.

I believe that each one of us could learn how to think differently. You are a "gifted and talented" child in God's Kingdom. You can come up with the answers to difficult questions. You don't have to have every answer today in this changing world. Part of our anxiety comes in "not knowing" an answer, or in anticipating the need to understand a hard question of life. However, you and I can think the way that God thinks.

If you trust in your own knowledge, you will miss the mark. You can be in harmony with God, however, and your spirit will bear witness to His Spirit of life. If you abide in Him, then you will be like Him! The world will see Him again today, just as it saw Him when He came and then manifested His Messiahship!

Abide in His presence and change the world around you!

QUESTIONS FOR ABIDING DEEPER

- What personal disciplines have you incorporated into your days that help you avoid distractions, stay focused on God, and abide in His presence?
- Does rest make your "Top 10" as you follow God's commands? (If not, make some course corrections in this area!) What effect does following His command to rest have on you?

- When faced with a question in life that needs an answer, what steps do you take to abide and align your thoughts with God's thoughts?

NOTES

Chapter 1 The War to Abide

1. Chuck D. Pierce and Rebecca Wagner Sytsema, *Possessing Your Inheritance: Take Hold of God's Destiny for Your Life* (Minneapolis: Chosen Books, 2009), 218.

2. Chuck D. Pierce and Pamela J. Pierce, *One Thing: How to Keep Your Faith in a World of Chaos* (Shippensburg, PA: Destiny Image, 2006), 103–104.

Chapter 3 Receiving His Favor

1. This definition of a stethoscope can be found on a number of medical information and study sites.

Chapter 7 Seeking God's Face

1. See, for example, the entries for *darash* in the *Brown-Driver-Briggs Hebrew and English Lexicon*, as well as various online lexicons.

2. Alexander Macalister, "Hunger," in *The International Standard Bible Encyclopedia*, vol. 3, ed. James Orr et al. (Chicago: The Howard-Severance Company, 1915), 1440.

3. Food and Agriculture Organization of the United Nations, *FAO Statistical Yearbook 2012: Part 2 Hunger Dimensions*, 88, https://www.fao.org/3/i2490e/i2490 e02a.pdf.

4. Food and Agriculture Organization of the United Nations, *An Introduction to the Basic Concepts of Food Security*, 2008, https://www.fao.org/3/al936e/al936e00 .pdf.

Chapter 8 Seeking God's Presence

1. *Christianity Today*, endorsing Eric Metaxas in *Bonhoeffer: Pastor, Martyr, Prophet, Spy* (Nashville: Nelson Books, 2010, 2020), ii.

2. H. Fischer-Hüllstrung in Metaxas, *Bonhoeffer*, 532.

3. Franklin Graham, *Rebel with a Cause: Finally Comfortable Being Graham, an Autobiography* (Nashville: Thomas Nelson, 1995), 119–120.

Chapter 9 Becoming His VIP

1. *Oxford Learner's Dictionaries*, s.v. "VIP," https://www.oxfordlearnersdiction aries.com/us/definition/english/vip?q=VIP.
2. *Oxford Learner's Dictionaries*, s.v. "identity," https://www.oxfordlearnersdiction aries.com/us/definition/english/identity?q=identity.
3. Blue Letter Bible, s.v. "katartizō" (Strong's G2675), accessed June 30, 2023, https://www.blueletterbible.org/lexicon/g2675/kjv/tr/0-1/.

Chapter 12 Dream to Make History

1. Robert H. Belton, s.v. "Dream," *Wycliffe Bible Encyclopedia*, eds. Charles F. Pfeiffer, Howard F. Vos, and John Rea (Chicago: Moody Press, 1975).

Chapter 17 Stake Your Claim from Your Abiding Place

1. *American Dictionary of the English Language* (San Francisco: Foundation for American Christian Education, 1987), s.v. "atmosphere."
2. Kimberly Daniels, *Give It Back!: God's Weapons for Turning Evil to Good* (Lake Mary, FL: Charisma House, 2007), 168.
3. Dutch Sheets, *Authority in Prayer: Praying with Power and Purpose* (Minneapolis: Bethany House, 2006), 24–25.
4. Geoffrey W. Dennis, *The Encyclopedia of Jewish Myth, Magic and Mysticism* (Woodbury, MN: Llewellyn Publications, 2007), 58.
5. Derek Prince, *Blessing or Curse: You Can Choose* (Minneapolis: Chosen, 2006), 45.
6. Jeff A. Benner, "The Aaronic Blessing from a Hebrew Perspective," Ancient Hebrew Research Center, accessed June 30, 2023, https://www.ancient-hebrew.org /studies-interpretation/aaronic-blessing-from-a-hebrew-perspective.htm.
7. Christian Answers, s.v. "Who Is King David?," last modified December 27, 2022, http://www.christiananswers.net/dictionary/david.html.
8. For more on this, see Leen and Kathleen Ritmeyer, *From Sinai to Jerusalem: The Wanderings of the Holy Ark* (Jerusalem: Carta, 2000), 52–57.
9. John Dickson, personal communication dated April 19, 2007.

Chapter 18 Abide and Be Transformed

1. Donald S. Whitney, *Spiritual Disciplines for the Christian Life* (Colorado Springs: NavPress, 1991), 67.
2. Bible Tools, s.v. "perispao" (Strong's 4049), https://www.bibletools.org/index .cfm/fuseaction/Lexicon.show/ID/G4049/perispao.htm.
3. Discovery Bible, s.v. "3309. merimnaó," Bible Hub, 2021, https://biblehub .com/greek/3309.htm.
4. Bible Hub, s.v. "3318. yatsa," accessed June 30, 2023, https://biblehub.com /hebrew/3318.htm.

5. This section on rest is adapted from pages 155–156 of my book coauthored with Rebecca Wagner Sytsema, *Possessing Your Inheritance: Take Hold of God's Destiny for Your Life* (Chosen, 2009).

6. Cindy Jacobs, "The Sabbath's Rest," *G. I. News* 4, no. 1 (1995): 1.

7. Jacobs, "The Sabbath's Rest," 1.

Charles D. "Chuck" Pierce leads an apostolic and prophetic ministry in Corinth, Texas. He is the president of Glory of Zion International and Kingdom Harvest Alliance. These ministries are housed at Global Spheres Center, which also includes Beulah Acres and the Israel Prayer Garden. He continues to gather and mobilize the worshiping Triumphant Reserve throughout the world. The ministries located at Global Spheres Center participate in regional and national gatherings to develop new Kingdom paradigms.

Dr. Pierce also serves as a key bridge between Jews and Gentiles as the Lord raises up One New Man. He is known for his accurate prophetic gifting, which helps direct nations, cities, churches, and individuals in understanding the times and seasons in which we live. He has written numerous bestselling books, and he has a degree in business from Texas A&M University, has done master's work in cognitive systems with the University of North Texas, and has a D.Min. from the Wagner Leadership Institute.

Chuck and his wife, Pam, have six children and many grandchildren.

🅕 ChuckDPierce

🆇 @ChuckDPierce

🅞 @ChuckDPierce

Dr. Alemu Beeftu, founder and president of Gospel of Glory, has traveled globally for decades, training and equipping Christian leaders to foster sustainable societal changes for the Kingdom of God.

He presently works with transformational leaders of various ages in more than fifty countries who have the calling, gifting, and character to foster such changes. He has a heart for training pastors, business-men, and politicians, with a goal of building national leadership infrastructures.

Dr. Beeftu earned a B.A. from Biola University, and master's and doctoral degrees in curriculum design and community development from Michigan State University. More than thirty years of practice in these and related fields have made him an accomplished and sought-after leadership trainer. He also continues to provide leader-ship worldwide for the Body of Christ. His most recently authored books include *The King's Signet Ring, Rekindle the Altar Fire, Optimize Your Potential, Go Back to Go Forward,* and *Breakout for Breakthrough.*

Alemu and his wife, Genet, and their family make their home in Highland Village, Texas. Learn more at www.GoGlory.org.